To, .CHR...
FROM, GR...

CW00324532

DIY
Tips

DIY

Tips

DIY
Tips

Frank Preston

mustard

This edition is published by Mustard 1999

Mustard is an imprint of Parragon

Parragon
Queen Street House
4 Queen Street
Bath BA1 1HE
UK

Printed and bound in Italy

© Central Press Features Ltd/ Arcturus Publishing Ltd

ISBN 1 84164 261 4

Tracy Batty

ABOVE AND BELOW THE CLOUDS

AUSTIN MACAULEY
PUBLISHERS LTD.

A CIP catalogue record for this title is available from the British Library.

ISBN 978 184963 932 3

www.austinmacauley.com

First Published (2014)
Austin Macauley Publishers Ltd.
25 Canada Square
Canary Wharf
London
E14 5LB

Printed and bound in Great Britain

Acknowledgments

The support and love of my children and grandchildren who I am immensely proud of.

Chapter One

Life at home

It was March 1940 and I was working in a shop at the top of Soaphouse Hill, It sold virtually everything from cotton to corned beef. One side sold household goods and food the other was a butcher's counter.

I worked on the household side and Mr & Mrs Sykes worked on the butcher's counter. I met the Sykes when I was at school I was best friends with Lily their daughter. Lilly had a brother John. He joined up as soon as war broke out and was in France.

"Hi, Lilly, didn't know you were helping out in shop today?"

"Yep not working so I said I would then Mum and Dad could have a lay in. We had a letter from John today first in ages."

"How is he?"

"Alright but it really upsets Mum after reading his letters."

Lilly worked at a mill near Huddersfield making uniforms for the soldiers.

"It's weird making all those uniforms knowing where they will end up."

"Well at least you're doing your bit for the war."

"Hey, Jenny, how about going out tonight there's a dance on at Unity Hall, It would cheer us both up and it is your birthday next week and it would get us out of the village for one night."

"Alright I don't finish till 5.30 so I'll catch the seven o'clock bus at the bottom of the hill and you can catch it at the top."

"Alright."

"Morning, Mrs Willis, how are you today?"

"Fine thanks, Jenny love, how's your Mum, Is she alright?"

"Yes fine thanks; what can I get you today?"

"Well I'll have to have some butter, flour, and dried eggs thanks, love. I've got a cake to bake."

"Have you got your ration books please?"

"Here you go that's me spent up for a while."

We didn't do too badly at the shop as we were quite near to the country and Mr & Mrs Sykes have friends nearby with quite large gardens. He bought fruit and veg that their friends had surplus of and bought rabbits and sometimes chickens from other people in the village.

"Hi girls you had a busy day?"

"Well, this morning but it went quiet this afternoon. Had a good day with Mum?"

"Yes it was nice to spend some time together but your Mum's still got that bad cough."

"Is it alright if I go now, Mr Sykes? Me and Lilly are going to the dance at Unity Hall tonight."

"Well alright but you two take care and be in by 10.30, Lilly."

"Dad."

"Lilly."

"Alright, but John was allowed."

"Lilly, I won't say it again, you know I like you in before I go to bed."

"Morning, Jenny."

"Morning, Lilly how are you today, Lilly? Lilly, what's wrong, are you alright?"

Lilly started to cry and reached for a handkerchief to wipe her eyes.

"Don't, Jenny, your setting me off again I can't let Dad see me crying. He will be suspicious and want to know why."

"What do you mean?"

"It's Mum."

Lilly's Mum sometimes coughed up blood but was keeping this from the family.

"When I was doing the washing yesterday I found blood all over her nightdress and some of her handkerchief. She's coughing up blood."

"Oh my Goodness, Lilly you must tell your Dad"

"I can't, I don't think he will cope."

"Look I'll send Mum up and ask her to have a word with her and try to get her to go the doctor."

"Alright, thanks, Jenny."

Mum came up the next day when Mr Sykes was out getting more veg from one of his friends; Lilly was at work and I was trying to cope on my own which wasn't easy. Mum came from out back after seeing Mrs Sykes. It was heaving by then and people were getting impatient as I was trying to work both counters.

"Do you want me to give you a hand while Mr Sykes gets back, love?"

"That would be great, Mum."

We worked all afternoon and Mr Sykes didn't get back till after five he had called in the New Inn before going for the veg and that's always a mistake when he gets in there with his buddies. He apologised and asked what Mum was doing there. I quickly said, "She came up for a rabbit for Dad's tea and it was busy and she gave me a hand."

"Oh that's very kind of you, Mrs Reed."

"That's fine but I'll have to go and get Bill's tea on."

"Here you go, some veg for your trouble."

Mrs Sykes told Mum everything and promised to go to see Dr Jacobs the next week. April was a great month. The weather was good for the time of year it was strange as sometimes you forgot there was a war on.

My twin brothers enlisted in the RAF and were waiting to go to RAF Catterick to do their training, Mum wasn't happy but she knew if they didn't enlist they would be called up anyway and this way they would at least be together and doing what they would prefer.

"Tom, Tim is waiting, you're going to miss the train."

"Coming, sis."

"Well you look so grown up, my boys."

"Mum we're nearly 21 you know."

"Have you got everything, Tom?"

"Yes, thanks, Tim."

"Well come on were going to miss the bloody train."

"Keep your hat on."

"Now make sure you look after each other. Write and keep safe."

Mum began to cry and the boys put their arms around her. She looked so small between them.

"Ann come on love let them go, come on love."

The days after Tom & Tim went were very sombre and very quiet. I noticed a big change in Mum and Dad the war had finally come to our house and changed everything. The boys wrote regularly and were full of everything that was happening. They had never gone anywhere before. The furthest they had gone was Wakefield so this was a big deal for them and their world had totally changed.

"Jenny, Jenny, Lilly's here."

"Alright, Mum. Hi, Jenny, how's things?"

"Alright, how's your Mum, is she feeling any better?"

"No not really, Dad's trying to get John home to see her. She's having more tests at the hospital tomorrow."

"Are you going?"

"Yes that's what I came to ask; if you and your Mum would mind the shop? Dad wants to come too would that be alright?"

"Yes course we'll be there at 7.30."

"Thanks."

Mum made some fresh bread and sent it home with Lilly and a rabbit casserole.

"Thanks, Mrs Reed, Mum will appreciate that."

They went to Clayton Hospital and they took Mary into a side room, more blood was taken and other tests done, they all waited in the waiting room for nearly three hours.

"Mrs Sykes."

"Yes."

"Can you come this way the doctor will see you now."

They all went in to the consultation room.

"I'm afraid it's bad news, Mrs Sykes, you've got tuberculosis and it is in the latter stages and there's nothing we can do, it's just a matter of time."

Mr Sykes turned to his wife and took hold of here she went all limp and began to cry. Lilly just sat there not taking it in just remembering all that was around her and what was in the room. It was shock she was suffering from they came out of the office and hugged each other.

The Sykes came into the shop and Mr & Mrs Sykes went upstairs and Lilly came over to me and burst into tears. She told us what they said and that there was no hope and that it wouldn't be long, she was in the latter stages. I worked more and more and Lilly had to stop working at the factory her Mum needed 24 hour care and she didn't come downstairs. She was hardly eating and was getting weaker and weaker and then one Saturday morning.

"Morning, Jenny, have you got a pound of potatoes and a couple of those leeks."

"Yes of course, I suppose Mr Wilkinson will be having leek and potato soup today."

"Yes, dear, it's his favourite and I'll do him some fresh bread."

"You spoil him you know."

"Well you'll be married one day and you will realise a way to a man's heart is his stomach."

I laughed. "I'll never get married."

Bang crash.

"What on earth was that, Jenny?"

"I don't know it came from upstairs."

The door flung open it was Lilly hysterical and trying to talk.

"Sit down," I said. "I can't understand what you're saying."

"Mum, it's Mum."

I held Lilly in my arms. The bang was Mary falling out of bed knocking the wash basin over. She was trying to get help with her last breath.

"She's died, she's died!" Lilly said.

Mrs Wilkinson went and got doctor Jacobs. Mr Sykes came in from out back after hearing the commotion he took one look at Lilly and knew what had happened.

"No, no; not my Mary!"

He ran upstairs. Soon after the doctor arrived and went up. I thanked Mrs Wilkinson and closed the door behind her and put the closed sign up. Working at the shop was quite hard after that, the sadness was all around. Things Mrs Sykes used to do and signs she had written. It was very hard on Lilly John couldn't get back for the funeral and a lot was left to Lilly. The war in France wasn't going well and Lilly hadn't heard from John in weeks. I was beginning to get really disheartened with my job, my life, about not having contributed to the war effort, and with everything that was happening in France; I felt I had to do something. Then something happened to change my plans for the time being anyway. Lilly was serving at the meat counter, I was at the other and Mr Sykes was outside cleaning the windows of the shop. A boy came up to Mr Sykes and handed him a telegram I looked at Lilly and she looked at her Dad. Mr Sykes just stood there and stared at the boy. I quickly finished serving and ushered the people out of the shop.

My heart was racing and I went outside and took Mr Sykes's arm and led him into the shop, Lilly came from behind the counter and took her Dad's hand. They looked at each other and the telegram.

"Can you read it, Jenny?"

"Me? No, no."

"Please, we need you to do this for us."

I took the telegram from Mr Sykes's hand. I opened it, my heart was pounding. I could feel sweat running down my face. I felt sick, how could I read this to Lilly and her Dad who had already been through so much; to have this as well. I began to read the telegram.

"I write to inform you that corporal John Sykes has been injured in battle on the Dunkirk beaches on May 29th 1940."

I couldn't read any more for the tears in my eyes I could hear Lilly shouting to her Dad, "He's alive, he's alive, Dad!"

He was in a military hospital and badly injured but he was alive. Mum came to the shop to help out wile Lilly and her Dad went down to see John, after a few days they were back.

"Morning Lilly, how did it go? How is he?"

"Well he looked battered and bruised He has some memory loss and then there's his leg. Well he lost the leg from the knee down. It's going to take time. He will be in hospital for a while then a convalescence home."

"Yes, but he's still alive. When I opened that telegram ... "

"I know, I think I stopped breathing"

The next couple of months passed quickly. I was at the shop quite a lot as Lilly and her Dad visited John. He was making good progress and had been moved to the convalescence home for wounded soldiers.

Lilly told me he had met a girl. Volunteers came in and read letters to them and took them out for walks and so on. Betty Newton was the youngest daughter of Seth Newton he owned the pub round the corner from the convalescence home. There were five sisters some were in the forces and one ran the pub with her Dad. Betty was the youngest she always felt inadequate and a surplus, her Dad wanted a boy and kept going but ended up with five girls.

Betty started to go and volunteer to help with the wounded soldiers because her Dad didn't want her round the pub He said, "Daddy's little girl wasn't working in the pub."

She didn't get to do everything. The others could do what they wanted. Betty started to take John out in a chair and to the pub to meet her Dad. They began to spend lots of time with each other and John asked her out and she said yes. Her sisters were happy for Betty but her Dad wasn't. He wanted better for his little Betty, but as Seth got to know John he mellowed and gave his blessing for them to see each other. John was discharged from the convalesced home and the army, he went round to the pub and asked Betty to marry him.

"Jenny, I'm going down to see John with Dad and I'm going to be his bridesmaid He's getting married and he's got a false leg so he will able to walk down the aisle."

"A false leg; slow down; I cannot take it all in he's getting married and has a false leg?"

"Yes, it's great isn't it?"

"That's good. Where they going to live, Lilly?"

"Well that's the best thing, they're coming back to Walton and living with us."

Well it was the best news for Lilly but if Betty and John came I don't see me having my job for much longer.

Betty came to Walton and she was a lovely girl, John was very quiet compared to what he was like when we were kids, but him and Betty seemed so in love, Mr Sykes was happy having John home and Lilly was getting back to her normal self. The pressure was off her shoulders. I felt more and more out of place at the shop and needed something more. The letters from Tom & Tim talked of camaraderie and I felt like I needed to do my bit, for the war. The first year of the war hadn't really brought much change to my life but there were letters from my brothers and seeing John with his injuries, so as the winter of 1940 approached it was time I made some changes.

Chapter Two

Joining up

It was October 1940 that I volunteered for the Women's Land Army I had read in the newspaper that thousands of women were urgently needed to work on the land and so I wrote off I was surprised to find I had to go to London Oxford street, for the interview. I arranged for a day off finding it hard to keep it from Lilly and Mum and Dad but just about managed it I caught an early train from Wakefield. When I arrived I was shown into a big office, in it was a large desk and there were wooden panels all around the room. A very smart looking woman came in and sat behind the desk she wore a beautiful silk dress and silk scarf. She began to twirl a gold pen continuously in her long fingers. She fired a barrage of questions at me. She made me feel very nervous. She wanted to know if I thought the land Army was all about feeding chickens and enjoying lovely weather.

"I've been potato picking."

I said (I've been potato picking – what was I saying?) that didn't impress her at all. I left the interview thinking that's that, so I was elated when I received a letter to say I had been accepted.

I had to be at Wakefield station on October 14th. Now the next worrying hurdle was to tell Mum and Dad the news and the Sykes. It was going to be hard.

"Hello, Betty, is Mr Sykes in?"

"Yes he's out back with John sorting out the veg and rabbits he just been and collected, you alright?"

"Yes but I've got to give notice I'm going in the Land Army next week."

"Good for you."

"What do you think they will say?"

"They will be sorry to lose you especially now I'm expecting and won't be able to do much, but they will be pleased for you, what's your family said?"

"I've not told them yet."

"Oh!"

"I am going to do that tonight over tea."

"Hello, Jenny, didn't think you were in today, everything alright?"

"Yes thanks can I have a quick word?"

"Of course, love, Lilly, put the kettle on."

Mr Sykes was great he was so excited about Betty and John's baby. He gave me a hug and told me to take the rest of the week off with pay and sort everything out with Mum and Dad.

"Jenny, did I hear you right, you have joined the Land Army?"

"Well, yes I was going to tell you but how I was going to do it well, we have been best friends for years and we have never been apart. I will really miss you."

"No, you're so lucky, you know, I have wanted to get out of this place for years."

"I know that's why I thought I would ask you to join up, too."

"I would love too, but what with the baby and Dad's health hasn't been good since Mum died."

"Well I better get back home and tell Mum and Dad, not looking forward to that."

"We will see each other before you leave won't we?"

"Of course we will."

Dad hit the roof and asked what I was thinking of leaving the family. In those days nobody left home, families looked after each other.

"But there's a war on, Dad, I want to go."

I explained that for a 48 hour week I would get one shilling per hour. Money was always important to my Dad because money had always been very thin on the ground. I continued on that I would pay twenty-five shillings for my billet. Another explosion came from Dad. Mum looked very unhappy. So with misery on one hand and a feeling of excitement on the other I looked forward to going to Elvington. This would be a big change having spent most of my life living in a small village with my Mum, Dad and my brothers.

"Lilly."

"Hello, Jenny, how are you? Are you ready for your big adventure?"

"Yes just the matter of our girl's night out."

"Alright where are we going?"

"Well there's a dance on in Crofton on Saturday night. There's a load of lads joining up from there and I've been sort of seeing one of them, Steve Yates."

"You never said."

"He worked at the farm at the top of the hill. I met him when I used to call up for potatoes for the shop. I've kept it from everyone then Dad didn't get to know he would never approve."

"That's great, but I am sorry he's going in the army."

"Well he could have stayed, but all his pals were joining up so he did."

We had a great night with Steve and his pals. We danced like we had never danced before. Then we went home and had a good night's sleep as I would be busy the next day getting ready to leave. After a teary goodbye, I picked up my case and went outside. It was a cold October morning and I made my way to Wakefield train station. I had to catch a train to York. When I arrived there were some twelve young women turned up at the station. They were from Wakefield, Manchester and Hull. We were met by a Women's Institute lady with a clip board. Four of us were billeted with Mrs Bell (Pat) at Sutton-on-Derwent, A nice little village near Elvington. We were in the same billet all the time. Billets were people's homes that volunteered to have us and we paid for our keep. Mrs Bell was a lovely, homely lady, a widow with three sons. There was a kind of hostility in the village. Servicemen were accepted, but not the land girls, so it was very brave of people like Mrs Bell to take us in. The general opinion held was that land girls wore too much in winter and too little in summer.

My uniform consisted of corduroy breeches, strong brown leather shoes, long woollen socks, fawn cotton aertex T-shirt, fine cotton long-sleeved fawn shirt with a band at the waist, a fawn felt hat with a women's land army badge, dark green tie, a dark green woollen jumper, pair of gun boots two light overall coats and a dark green oilskin. It really hit me the first morning when we were told to meet a lorry at 6.30 in the village. It was dark, very dark I felt cold and tired; I was convinced the village clocks had been tampered with. I had to break the ice in the jug before washing. My oil skin jacket crackled and smelt of disinfectant. I wore umpteen layers everything I could get my hands on, I could hardly walk.

Another fourteen girls were picked up in the lorry and we travelled fast along a dark country lane. It was bending from side to side then came to a sudden stop, skidding in the mud on the road. I was daydreaming, thinking I was still in my warm bed back at Mrs Bells. I shared my room with three other girls Sally, Marge and Dolly. Pat Bell was a widow; her husband was killed at Dunkirk. She had three sons; Tony the eldest, he was twenty, Mark fourteen, and Philip twelve. She had made us all feel very welcome when we were all away from our homes. We came to an abrupt stop. We all fell forward and I jumped out of my daydream I heard the driver shout out my name and Dolly's. We jumped out of the back of the lorry and he told us to walk to the bottom of the lane and knock on the door. Mr and Mrs Baker, George and Gaynor will be there. We walked into a muddy yard with a straw shed at one side and the house on the other.

"Dolly, knock on the door."

Dolly was from Hull, another Yorkshire girl, but had never been on a farm. She was slim with long auburn hair and was quite chatty and easy to get on with. Gaynor opened the door and in a strong Welsh accent said, "Come in girls get a warm by the fire."

Gaynor was quite a small lady with short hair, she had met George when he went down to Wales on a family holiday. She later moved up to Yorkshire and was married to George. She seemed a very friendly person. George came in and introduced himself and asked Gaynor to make a cuppa before he took us up to the field. George and Gaynor were quite a young couple to be well established in farming, but George's Dad, George Senior, had died of pneumonia in 1937, so George had to take over. George's Mum Edith, still lived with them. They had two young girls, Millie 9, Jill 7, and they were both so very different, Millie was a real girl's girl and didn't like getting dirty on the farm; she spent a lot of the time with her gran, Edith. Jill was opposite, always with her Dad, getting into everything she shouldn't and was always in the muck.

I expect their thoughts were mixed when they saw us two townie girls around five feet two inches and weighing eight stone. They must have thought they'll not last. They were wrong we tackled all the jobs, although I expect Dolly hadn't seen a spade let alone used one. Mr Baker took us up to the top field. He heaved up a huge sugar beet in each hand clutching the leaves the beets were as big as our heads.

The idea was to bang them together and toss them neatly in a row minus soil. We set off Dolly nearly sank without a trace having staggered to the end of two rows. I stood up with difficulty I thought my back was broken and that it would never mend. Was my Dad right? Should I have stayed at home?

George showed us how to handle a bill-hook, a strong wooden handle supporting a short curved blade with which we had to take the tops off, Dolly really got the hang of it and was going through them as quick as anything. The field was massive and it took some three weeks to clear. By the end we expertly tossed the sugar-beet into a small horse-drawn waggon then we bagged the beet for market.

Meanwhile I wrote home to say everything was lovely and that I had settled in with a good family. I was good friends with the girls I shared my billet with, especially Dolly who worked with me at the Baker's farm. Mum wrote back quite often keeping me informed of all the goings on back home in Walton, John and Betty's baby was due in June and Mum said

John was much stronger now and Betty had settled in well. It would be strange being away from home for Christmas but I would be with very good friends and the Bakers.

The Bell's boys were also very lively and Pat had her hands full especially with Mark and Philip as they had got a bit out of hand after their Dad was killed. He volunteered to join up straight away after war broke out; he died on the beaches with hundreds of other soldiers. Tony on the other hand had his mind set on going in the RAF He was always asking me questions about Tom and Tim they were both flying Bombers by now and that's just what Tony had in mind, he couldn't talk to Pat about it, not as she was still very upset about John, her husband, but as Tony knew he would be called up soon anyway. He wanted to be the one making decisions about what he was going to be doing. Tony was all set to enlist after Christmas and was waiting to put it all in motion but wanted to spend a happy Christmas with his family. Like my brothers he would do his basic training at the Cattrick Barracks.

Back to Christmas 1940, it was cold and we were up early to help milk the cows. Usually George and Gaynor did it but we all went in that morning to get it done. Milking made my wrist ache, and after all that we had to carry buckets of milk to feed the calves before finally carrying the heavy churns to the end of the lane to stand them on the stone table for them to be collected.

You soon learnt to stay clear of the cows' tails as they swished and really stung when they hit you in the face, very smelly too.

We finished at 8.30 and Gaynor had made us breakfast.

"Hi, Gaynor, that smells great. Where's the girls?"

"Already dressed and in the parlour playing with their new dolls."

"Dolly, do you want toast or have you had enough?"

"Well I shouldn't, but your butter is the best."

"You'll never get in that new dress you bought."

We finished breakfast and made our way back to Pat's to enjoy a family Christmas with the Bell family. Tony was very quiet and you could see he was wrestling with his conscience.

Pat had embroidered all us girls handkerchiefs for Christmas and we got Pat some lavender soap and a paste broach that Sally and Marge found on a market stall in York.

"Oh, girls, you shouldn't have, they're lovely, I can't remember when I last had real soap to use."

Mark and Philip and George made a new linen basket up at the farm out of reed from the local pond.

"You two made it. I cannot believe it. Together, you two?"

"Well George showed us how. He made one for Gaynor."

We had a quiet day and it was nice to just do nothing George and Gaynor were doing the evening milking and we were having a well-earned night off.

"Sally you ready yet? I need to get in the bathroom. It's nearly 6.30."

"Sorry just trying to get the pig smell out of my hair."

All us girls were going in to Elvington to a New Year's Eve dance.

"Jenny, have you got the pencil for my seam down my leg? I'm about ready."

"Yep give me a minute. I'll come and do it for you."

We all caught the bus from Sutton-on-Derwent to Elvinton. There was an air base in Elvinton but it was only a grass airfield at the time but there were still some RAF based there so there was some good looking lads at the dance. Dolly wore her new dress and even though she had eaten very well over the Christmas period it still fitted her great. Later on the way home from the dance.

"I wish we had gone for the last bus. My feet are killing me."

"Stop moaning, Marge you weren't saying that when you were dancing round the floor with that RAF guy."

"Come on we have all got to get up for work tomorrow."

We made our way back to Pat's and to our lovely comfy beds. We all hoped 1941 would bring an end to this war.

Chapter Three

Our Farming Year

The beginning of the year was cold and we still all had our jobs to do but the weather made all of them that much harder. I had chilblains on top of chilblains and my fingers were red with the cold. After breakfast we fed all the animals, the pigs and the cows. The girls did the chickens before they went to school and when they got back and would put them away to keep them safe from the foxes. Our jobs were many and varied and by March we were preparing to plough the fields and plant crops. George was teaching Dolly and I how to drive the old Ford tractor. He also taught us to do our own maintenance for if it broke down in a field away from the farm. It was a difficult task when we had to crank the old tractor on a frosty morning in winter as the Fordson had no self-starter. When it had been standing out in an open field all night, it certainly took a lot of muscle to get it going again.

"Dolly, give us a hand with this bloody tractor. We need to get going before George gets up here."

"You get in the seat, Jenny, and I'll give it a go."

The old tractor roared into action.

"Great, Dolly, you did it!"

"Well it's all those breakfasts Gaynor makes me."

"Ha, ha, ha!"

"Come on you two, you have work to do. There's the oats to do this week and barley next."

"Jenny's going first."

"Well you can follow me and we'll do some stone picking. We'll swap over at lunch."

It was great on the tractor but you had to really concentrate to keep the plough in the furrow.

"Gaynor, you're a site for sore eyes. Food is just what me and the girls need."

"Well I thought you would be about ready."

We all had our food by the side of the tractor and when we had finished George and Gaynor went back to the farm to prepare for afternoon milking.

"You girls finish the ten acres and don't forget to swop placers. See you when you finish."

"Well at least I have the tractor this time. My back's killing me."

"Well let's get on before it starts to get dark."

At about 6pm we pulled in to the yard and washed down the tractor and plough.

"Hi, George, top ten all done and tractor away in the barn."

"Thanks girls have a lie in tomorrow and come for 7 and we can start on the next field of oats."

"Alright George see you tomorrow."

The next two weeks we worked hard to get the crops in and it was backbreaking. We were all ready for a few quiet weeks. I had a letter from Mam telling me that Lilly had joined the Air Force and was based in Catterick.

She was going to be flying planes up and down the country delivering new planes to our boys.

"Well I don't believe it, she really has gone and done it, got out of Walton."

"What?"

"Sorry."

"I was just thinking out loud my best friend Lilly from back home has joined the RAF and is delivering planes."

"Gosh how exciting, she must be very brave Jenny."

"Well maybe spontaneous, not so much brave. She has wanted to get out of our village since we were children."

I received a letter from Lilly, she had settled in and was doing her training and was really enjoying being up in the Spits as she called them now. She hoped to get to see me as they could be delivering some to Elvington but not until she had finished her training.

We planted the potatoes to be harvested mid-October and we did the hoeing in-between the plants. The weather was getting better and the crops were growing at a flourishing speed. The locals were amused by us townies which made us all more determined to show them we were made of sterner stuff. Tony Bell had left to do his training at the end of January and Pat had reluctantly accepted that Tony would have had to go to war and that it is what he wanted. We were so lucky living with Pat and her family. The cottage was quite large and Pat kept it really cosy it was always warm in the kitchen when we came home from a long day.

"Oh it's so good to be home. My feet are killing me."

"Me too, I think I'm going to soak them in a bowl of water."

"Good idea I'll have a go after you."

"Want some tea you two?"

"Oh that would be nice, Pat."

"Have you heard from Tony lately?"

"Yes he's relay enjoying being in a crew and making new friends."

"Tim and Tom said that they became close to the other men in their crew early on."

"Your turn, Dolly."

"Thanks, Jenny."

The summer was soon upon us. We were busy getting ready for the cows to calve before we got busy with all the harvesting in August, Lilly wrote and told me that Betty had had their baby a little girl that was the apple of old Mr Sykes eye and she had given him a new lease of life as he hadn't been very well through the winter. Lilly had Seen Tim and Tom on her travels. They both looked well and were trying to get some leave to get back and see Mum and Dad. It was summer time and we took the tractor up to the top ten, complete with the binder which Dolly sat on. We cut the ten acre field. It was a wonderful sight to see on a summer morning, the field full of golden crops waving and stretching out before me, and later in the afternoon to see it transformed in to a totally different place, it was so rewarding I loved that job.

The seasons began to fly by with all the work and it soon became threshing time. What a job that was. Dust and chaff everywhere, we put scarves on our heads to protect our hair but couldn't stop it going down our throats. The Threshing machine was a monster. It rattled and shook. It was attached to a steam engine by a big rubber band and it was dangerous. We had to be very careful. There were different jobs to be done so we changed around. There would be two of us on the rick throwing the sheaves up to the one on the machine who cut the bands and fed the wheat into the hole hoping you wouldn't fall.

"George, is that it, are we done?"

"Yes, Gaynor, all in and done for another year."

"Well we'll be off, George, see you in the morning."

"Alright, girls, get some rest. You deserve it."

The next year passed very quickly and we all settled into our jobs.

We felt like part of the Baker family it was quite a quiet place and everyone knew everyone else. We went to the local dances, but most of the boys were away fighting, but in October 1942 a lot changed at Elvington Airfield as it became operational.

Chapter Four

Elvington Bomber Command / The Wedding

The squadron moved in to Elvington Airfield, commencing intensive training in Halifax bomber aircraft in October 1942. The base was declared operational at the end of January.

"Jenny, have you heard about the squadron that's moved in to Elvington Airfield?"

"No when did that happen?"

"Well I gather they have been preparing for them for a while, they have put three new runways in."

"How do you now that?"

"Well Marge has been seeing that RAF lad she met at the dance, he's part of the radio ops on the base."

"Whatever 'appen'd to talk costs lives?"

"They never met Marge."

"Dolly."

This brought a big change to our social lives we had regular dances in the Village and through this Marge and Paul were getting closer. Paul brought all the new lads from the squadron to the dances at village hall Elvington. We got friends with quite a few of the lads but it was hard when you knew what they were going out to do and to risk. Most of their time was spent getting to know their new wing Commander and to commencing intensive training with their Halifax bombers.

"We're going out tonight to Elvington. There's a dance on, all the lads are going Paul said last night, you three coming?"

"Marge, you're seeing a lot of Paul."

"Well he is great in that uniform he wears."

"Dolly, come on, the time's ticking, were going to be late."

"Alright, Jenny, coming."

"Well, are you coming or what?"

"We'll see how we both feel when we get back, Marge."

"Bye, bye."

"Morning, George. All alright this morning?"

"Yes thanks, Jenny, just those five in the stalls left if you want to give us a hand."

"Yes, course I will. Any chance of a warm cow against me on a cold frosty morning?"

"Are you girls going to the dance tonight?"

"Well I said to Marge and Sally I'd see how tired we were."

"Dolly, put the kettle over the fire; they're on their way in."

"Will do."

"Jill, set the table, where's Millie?"

"She's just taken Gran her jug of water."

"Morning, Gaynor."

"Morning, Jenny. Sit straight down all nearly ready."

We sat at the table with all the Baker family. We had really got lucky being sent there, they treated us just like family.

"We'll clean the cattle shed out today girls I think we need more space for the cows that will be due to calve over the Christmas holidays."

"That's going to make it a lot easier when they do calve, its much nearer to get to them, George."

We moved all the cows in to the small paddock at the back of the house. Then cleaned out the shed Dolly and George brought straw from the barn. We spread it all around the cattle shed, and then put all the cows in together and fed them.

"Well that's a job well done, girls, now let's see to the rest of the stock before dinner."

On our way home and ready for our baths Dolly and I were deciding whether we would go to the dance or not.

"Well it's the last dance before the Christmas dance."

"I know we ought to make an effort really even though I would rather just fall into bed."

We got back to Pat's at about 6.30. Sally and Marge were already in the bathroom, getting really giddy by the sounds of it.

"You two sound full of it. Are you nearly done?"

"Yep nearly, Jenny, you two coming then?"

"If you two get out of there and let us get in."

It was a mad rush. We were all racing around the house as Paul would be here soon he was coming to pick up Marge, she said we would all have a lift as he was borrowing the truck.

"Hello Mrs Bell, is Marge ready."

"Come on in Paul and I've told you call me Pat."

"Sorry."

"I think you have a few more to collect than you thought all the girls are coming."

"That's great she has persuaded them then. The lads will be pleased."

We all set off in the truck, Marge in the front and me, Dolly and Sally in the back. It was hard to keep our balance in the back but it was better than walking in our heels. We soon arrived outside the Hall and Paul parked the truck at the back we all got out with great relief and made our way to the front of the Hall.

"Pete, Roddy, get some drinks in for the girls."

The boys whistled.

"Where did you find this bevy of beauties, Paul my boy?"

"I have my sources."

We grabbed a table at the front and the three boys brought some drinks. We quickly introduced ourselves and within minutes of the music starting up Marge was on her feet with Paul. There were many different coloured uniforms the blue of the RAF the main one, but also at Elvington were based Canadians, Australians and New Zealanders. The boys were very chatty. You could see they were happy just to be with us all at the dance. It was an honour to spend some time with such brave young boys.

"Hello I'm Dolly this is Jenny and the one on the end is Sally."

"Hi, girls, well, girls, you are a sight for sore eyes after spending weeks with this ugly lot."

"Ha, ha, ha!"

"Well you smell better than what we usually have to spend our time with."

"And what's that then, Jenny?" Pete asked.

"Cows."

"Well you're braver than me I wouldn't want to get too close to any end of a cow."

"It's quite good on a cold frosty morning as the cows are really warm."

"Well, Jenny, how would you like to spend some time next to me on the dance floor?"

"Alright."

I was a bit nervous dancing with Pete. He was very handsome and self-confident.

"What's wrong Jenny? Have I said anything I shouldn't?"

"No, no its just I'm not really a good dancer and I find it quite embarrassing."

"You're great, Jenny, don't sell yourself short you feel just fine to me."

Pete waltzed me round the room. After what he said I forgot what other people would think and just relaxed and started to enjoy myself.

"Where you from, Jenny, you're not local are you?"

"No, but I am from Yorkshire, a little place called Walton, I live with my parents and twin brothers Tim and Tom, but that was before the war."

"What they doing now?"

"Both on bombers coincidentally, so I worry about them both all the time."

"I can understand that. My Mum worries all the time about me and my brother who's in the army."

"Where are you from?"

"Well promise you won't hate me, Blackburn, I'm a Lancashire lad and I do remember doing about the War of the Roses in school but don't hold it against me."

"Ha, Ha!"

"Dad would love that; I'm dancing with a lad from Lancashire."

We spent most of the night dancing and Peter was very good company and the confidence he gave me on the dance floor was great. Paul gave us a lift back which was great because it had started to snow quite hard and it would be near on impossible to walk in our heels.

"Oh I cannot believe it's time to get up already."

"It was a good night though, Dolly, wasn't it?"

"Well you seemed to enjoy yourself. Pete kept you on the dance floor all night. I never seen you dance so much, I thought you weren't that keen on dancing."

"Well I suppose it's who you're dancing with."

I could feel the heat rise up my neck as I remembered dancing with Pete. As we made our way to the Bakers' farm Dolly and I discussed what we would be doing at work today. How the farm changed season by season and how our days were always so different.

"At least the snow's nearly gone at last."

"Hi Jenny, Dolly, we're going to see what the shops have in for Christmas, to find something for Mum and Dad."

"You're lucky wish I was coming. Have a good day girls."

"Just seen the girls with Edith on the lane both very excited, doesn't seem a year since last Christmas, this year has gone so quickly."

"When I first married George I used to think that. It's all the seasons; they are so busy with things that we have to do. They seem to flow into each other and rush the year through."

"I know with the girls going Christmas shopping it's made me think I better get something started as there isn't much in the shops this year."

"Hi, Jenny, Mum's out but she said to tell you there's a couple of letters on the mantelpiece."

"Great thanks, Philip."

I went upstairs and took off my outer clothes and started to fill the bath. It always felt great being in the bath after being so dirty and smelly all day even if it wasn't as full as I would like it.

"Done in the bathroom if anyone wants it."

"Thanks Jenny."

I went into our room and put my slippers on and dressing gown, sat on my bed. I opened the first letter and it was from my best friend Lilly.

Dear Jenny

Great news I have had some promotion and I'm really enjoying being in the sky. I see quite a lot of the twins now especially Thomas, well actually quite a lot Of Thomas and we have been going out for about three months I should have told you sooner but I thought I better wait to see if anything came of it. Please don't be cross try and be happy for us this war is changing everything and with Thomas being in bomber command well he's asked me to marry him and I've said yes. Please write back soon I want you to be there. We've got leave next week and are trying to organise it for then it will only be a registrar office do.

Your very best friend
Lilly

Well I couldn't believe it where had that come from? Out of the blue I would say. The other letter was from my brother Tom saying virtually the same as Lilly's.

"What's up, Jenny, you look a bit shocked?"

"Well my brother is about to marry my best friend, Lilly and I didn't even know they were seeing each other."

"Are you pleased about it?"

"Shocked, but pleased about it. I need to ask George about going home next week they're having a quick registrar office do."

A travel warrant was arranged and it seems strange when I boarded the train in York. I was going home to Wakefield the village that I was brought up in, both the twins would be at home, Tim was going to be Tom's best man, Mam would be pleased that she was having us all at home at the same time since the twins joined up in 1940. I walked down our street and it looked so strange with all the taped windows sandbags, round the doors. I pulled the key through the letterbox, Mum kept the key on a string.

"Hello, hello is there any one in?"

"In here love, Jenny, you look great that country air really suits you."

"Hello, Dad. How you keeping? You've lost weight."

"It's all this rationing we have to put up with, girl, we're not all as lucky as you on the farm."

"No but I bought you some goodies that George and Gaynor have sent for the wedding."

"That's very decent of them, Jenny."

"They're really good people, Dad, I'm really happy there."

"Sis."

"Tom, you dark horse, you taking my best friend and marring her."

"Well it's the Reed family charm. What do you say, Tim?"

"Jenny, great to see you, as you can see our charming brother hasn't changed."

"Hey!"

Everything had been arranged for the next day at Wakefield register office at 12am. I was excited to see Lilly so I had tea with all my family then made my way up to the shop to the Sykes family. I knocked on the door.

"Jenny, Jenny, it's so good to see you, you look great."

"You, too."

"Come in, come in, John, Betty, it's Jenny."

The shop hadn't changed a bit except that the shelves had less on them. We sat round the fire and all caught up with what we had all been doing. Betty was expecting another baby in the summer. John and Betty were so proud of their little girl, Pauline, she was Grandad's little angel, Jack doted on her, she had been named after Lilly's Mum.

"Where's Mr Sykes, Lilly?"

"Dad's at the New Inn. He'll be back later and you better start to call him Jack as we'll be family from tomorrow."

"Give my love to Thomas won't you, Jenny?"

"Will do."

The next day was frantic; Mum fussing over the twins but Dad was just sat in the chair as usual smoking his pipe. There weren't too many people at the registrar office, just Thomas's crew and Lilly's family. We took two photos of the happy couple, both in uniform, and one of all of us which I was glad of, not knowing it would be the last time we would be together.

Chapter Five

Christmas 1942

On my journey back to Sutton-on–Derwent, It felt like I was going home. It had been great seeing all the family but I feel like I fitted in better on the farm than I ever did at home.

"Hello, love, you look done in, Philip, put the kettle on and make Jenny a cup of tea."

"Will do, Mam."

"Thanks, Pat, you are a life saver. It's great to be back."

"Did it all go alright at the wedding?"

"Yes quiet but it was great, it was the first time we were all together since the twins joined up."

"Bet your Mum and Dad were happy, having you all at home."

"Yes they were and Dad was very impressed with all the goodies George sent me with, especially the butter."

"That will please Gaynor."

"Thanks, Philip, that's a really good cuppa."

The hectic bustle of Christmas soon brought me back down to earth, at the farm we were sorting out the birds that would be going to be killed for Christmas.

"Well catch it, Dolly, don't just stand there."

Dolly screamed.

"You know I hate it when they flap at me, they know I am scared."

"Ha, ha!"

"Dolly, what you like?"

"George, George, don't catch the speckled one, Millie will be devastated," Edith said to her son.

"I won't, Mum, you get yourself inside. It's freezing out here."

We sorted out the hens and some cockerels. We had quite a few Cockerels and they were starting to fight so that would sort that out.

"I'll sort one out for Mrs Bell as she's quite a lot of you to feed."

"Thanks, George, that will please her she does struggle with rations, but it's much easier since you showed Mark and Philip how to do the veg patch."

"It all helps these days. Gaynor has been struggling to get the girls everything for Christmas we seem to have less and less every year."

I had already started this year as Mum had sent me back with two cardigans for the girls. She had pulled out one of my old ones and re knitted it, but as for the rest I will have to see if the girls at home want to come shopping to York on Saturday afternoon. George had said me and Dolly could have the afternoon off.

"Marge, you free Saturday afternoon, me and Jenny are going shopping to York?"

"Sorry, girls, but Paul is taking me out for the day. He says it's going to be special."

"Lucky girl."

"I'm free if I can tag on," shouted Sally.

"Yeah that's fine."

We got all the jobs done as soon as we could and back to Pat's for a wash and get changed. We were catching the 12.30 train to York.

"Do you think we should go and have a bit of lunch before we start I'm starving," Sally said.

"When are you anything else? Sally, you're as bad as Marge."

"Ha, ha!"

We all went into a small cafe and the girl came over for our order. We all had poached egg on toast and a mug of very weak tea.

"Think this tea was yesterday's washing up water, thank goodness for Pat Bell and her lovely food, and tea."

We made our way to the small market it had diminished over the time of the war, but you could still pick up a bargain now and again.

"We'll split up because I have your gifts to buy. Shall we meet back at the station to catch the 6.30 train? Is that alright with you two?"

"Yes fine, Jenny See you then."

I found Philip and Mark some socks not very exciting but practical, Clip on earrings made of paste for the three girls and a new pinny for Pat and Gaynor. I found some baccie for George I loved the smell, it reminded me of Dad. Edith's was my last present and I didn't know what to get her. Then I came across a stall selling the most lovely lace handkerchiefs and one had an E in the corner. That was it all done. Christmas can come now, I was ready. Back at the station the girls were all excited about the things that they had managed to get and were all very pleased with their purchases.

"Spent up, Jenny?"

"Not half, but really pleased with what I got."

"Me, too," said Sally.

"Are you two going to the Christmas Eve dance?"

"Think so, Peter has asked me to go."

"You going, Dolly?"

"Yes, Roddy asked me when we went to the last dance."

"That's great seems ages since we were all out together."

The next few days were hectic at the farm. We had three cows calve and one had twins, George was over the moon so that meant three more for milking. They weren't first calves so they knew what it's all about. Christmas eve we went up to the farm early to get all the jobs done I took all my presents and Gaynor was so pleased She quickly took them and put them in the sideboard in the parlour so the girls didn't see. We sat and had a great breakfast together, then back out to bed up the freshly calved cows and put out all the feed; Millie and Jill helped as they did when they were off school.

"Jill, have you seen the new calves? They are twins like your brothers, but they're girls."

"Yeah, Jill, I have. You will have to name them. Think of two names that go together."

"Well we have named the other two Dolly and Jenny after you two."

"Thanks, Jill, ha, ha!"

"It was Dad's idea."

"Oh was it now."

"I think we should pick something Christmassy, don't you?"

"That's a good idea; we'll all think hard about it and decide when we go in for dinner."

We cleaned out the pigs, fed them, and then we brought in the eggs with the girls and fed the chickens, swept the yard and stacked some more logs by the door for the fire.

"Dolly, take the slops out to the pigs, then you'd better all come for your dinner."

"Will do, Gaynor."

We all sat round the large wooden kitchen table and ate a lovely meat and veg pie, with potatoes with loads of gravy. We were so lucky to have Pat and Gaynor. We ate very well even though there was a war on.

"Well, girls, I would like to make a toast to thank you both for all your hard work for another year, Jenny, Dolly."

"They'll be a few additional jobs next year, I've bought some more sheep from someone Gaynor knows down in Wales and he's bringing them up between Christmas and New Year. They'll be new jobs to learn dipping, lambing and shearing."

"Great, George, I love sheep and all those baby lambs."

"Dolly, you do realise the lambs will be fattened and go to market."

"George," Gaynor said.

"Sorry, love."

Gaynor didn't like him to talk about things like that in front of the girls; Jill had nightmares and wouldn't go near the animals if she thought anything was going to happen to them.

"We'll I think you girls should decide what to call the twins."

"Well, Jill wants to call one Holly and I was thinking Ivy for the other one. It would remind us they were born at Christmas."

"Well, you girls better get off home. Me and Gaynor will do the evening milking, enjoy the dance, but be up here all the earlier the day after tomorrow."

"Thanks, George, Gaynor, bye, bye girls."

We quickly made our way back to Pat's and got in the bathroom before the other girls got back. We were well on our way to being ready before they got back.

"You got done early lucky buggers," Sally said.

"Can I come with you girls tonight? Paul is taking Marge to dinner first."

"Course you can, Sally, Paul's getting very romantic lately. Didn't think he had it in him."

"Hey that's my beloved you're talking about you lot."

"Ha, ha."

"You're coming later though, Marge, aren't you?"

"Yes course, save us some seats won't you."

We walked down to the Village Hall and I met Peter at the door.

"Hi, Jenny, you look great seems ages since we got a chance to spend some time together."

"You're right, but what with the wedding and sorting out the farm for Christmas."

"Come on, let's get some drinks and a table."

"We need to save a place for Marge and Paul. Do you know what he's up to with Marge taking her out for a romantic meal?"

"Well that would be telling, you'll have to wait and see."

"Peter."

"No sorry sworn to secrecy."

We were dancing for about an hour when Marge and Paul came in. Marge looked like she had been crying I thought something had gone wrong but on the contrary.

"Hi girls you got us a good table the. Were you early?"

"Yes got finished in really good time."

Sally squealed.

"Marge oh Marge."

"What's wrong Sally?" I said.

"Look at her left hand."

There was a tiny solitaire sitting and sparkling on her left hand we all squealed and ran and hugged Marge and Paul. They looked so happy together.

"Paul you old dog you," Dolly said.

We all continued to dance. Paul and Marge looked so happy in each other's arms. Peter and I were dancing very close together he then asked me to go outside for some fresh air. Peter got hold of my hand.

"I know you have had a lot on what with the wedding and now Paul and Marge, but I did intend to ask you this before all the excitement. Please don't think it's because of what's happened tonight."

"Come on, Peter, spit it out what's wrong?"

"Nothing's wrong it's just, I would like to ask you to be my girl and start courting I now it's a bit soppy but?"

"Oh, Pete, I would be proud to be your girl and courting is fine by me."

That was it we were a couple I had wanted this more than I realised, but when I was away I really did miss Peter so much.

It was Christmas morning and the smell of bird was wafting up the stairs. The girls were still sleeping it wasn't often we were all in bed at this time of the day. We had all come in late as we had all been celebrating Marge and Paul's good news. I got out of bed and washed quickly as it was cold I dressed and went downstairs to find Pat rushing round the kitchen and the table was covered in food.

"Morning, Pat."

"Oh hello, love, didn't expect you up yet."

"The others are all still sleeping. We had a great night Marge and Paul got engaged and Pete and I are courting."

"Well no wonder you were all in so late."

"Anything I can do to help?"

"Those sprouts our Mark has fetched in from the garden need doing if you don't mind."

"No problem, Pat."

We all sat round Pat's lovely laid table and enjoyed our Christmas dinner together.

"You go into the parlour, Pat, us girls will wash up and bring you a cuppa."

"Thanks girls."

We all went into the parlour where Mark had lit the fire. We all swapped Christmas presents and spent the rest of the day just relaxing and talking about Paul and Marge's engagement, and, of course, their up and coming wedding.

It was about 6.30 and there was a knock at the door.

"Who's that at this time of a night on Christmas Day?" Pat asked.

Philip went and answered the door and then made his way back to the parlour; there was someone standing behind him.

"It's someone for you, Jenny."

"Me?"

I stood up and walked towards the door and Philip moved to the side.

"Tim, what the heck you doing here?"

"That's a nice welcome for your big brother."

"Tim, Tim, it's great to see you, you alright?"

"Let him in, Jenny, he must be freezing."

"Thanks, I am a bit, I've been transferred to 77 squadron, I'm going to be flying Halifax four engine bombers, I'll be stationed in Elvington."

"Oh, Tim, that will be great I'll get to see more of you and you'll get to meet Peter. He's part of the 77 squadron."

"Who's Peter?"

"Well, he's my fella. We've just started courting."

"Well I'll have to check him out."

We all enjoyed some lovely cocoa before Tim made his way back to Elvington and we all went to bed.

Chapter Six

Squadron Goes Operational

More crews came to Elvington along with my brother Tim.
They soon had missions to fly. I worried a lot about the twins
but being so near to Elvington we heard the bombers going
out. We would wait till we heard them coming back and tried
to count them back in. On the fourth of February it was the
squadron's first raid using the Halifax bombers. It was over
Lorient, France quickly followed by several similar targets.

"How's your Tim getting on at the base, Jenny?"

"Good he's settled as well as you can in those
circumstances."

"Has he met Peter yet?"

"Yes they get on great, and with Paul and Roddy, there's a
new crew in this week," Peter said. "We're all going to the
dance to help them settle in."

Meanwhile back at Pat's she was worrying about her boys.
She already had Tony in the bombers. Mark was always
talking about only being three years till he can join up. Pat
hoped like the rest of us that it would be over by then. Tony
was based somewhere up country but we didn't get to know
where as "Talk costs lives" Pat has to write to him via his
regiment address.

Meanwhile back at the farm after Christmas.

"Dolly, Jenny, guess what we got at Christmas?"

"Well he isn't really ours, Jill."

"Yes but we can stroke him and take him for walks."

"Go on then tell us."

"A sheep dog, silly, he's not trained yet as he is only a
puppy."

"Dad says you haven't to make him soft, Jill, he has work
to do with the sheep."

"I know, I know don't be so bossy Millie."

"You alright, George."

"Yes thanks, now I've got the sheep in the top paddock. We're very lucky we've got the top paddock, it's too steep to be used for anything else."

"Heard you got yourself a collie to help with the sheep."

"Well eventually, as long as the girls leave him alone, we'll go up and see the sheep after breakfast. I want to check how many are in lamb then I can separate them in to the old barn later on."

"Alright I'll get on with feeding and bedding up."

"Thanks, Jenny."

"Dolly, can you see to the pigs, lass, then we can all go in to breakfast."

"Alright, George, will do."

"You've done well here, George, they look in good condition."

"Yes just need them to be in lamb then we will be busy at Easter."

We sorted out the ones in lamb and George was happy only five not in lamb, and then there's last year's lambs which will be put to the ram next year.

It was Saturday night. Paul collected us all from Pat's. The lorry was full of the boys from the base including Roddy, Tim and my lovely Peter and also the new crew.

"Hi, Jenny, let me give you a hand."

"Hi, Tim, you alright?"

"Yes, sis, just ready and willing to help all you lovely ladies in the back."

We all had a great time at the dance. Dolly was with Roddy most of the time, I was with Peter and of course Paul was with Marge. Tim was spreading himself around the single ladies dancing with all the pretty girls. The new crew seemed very young and so fresh-faced but we made them all welcome. We made our way home after the dance, not too late as we were all up early the next day.

"Come on, Sally, turn the light off I need some sleep."

"Alright, alright give me a minute."

"There I'm in bed; everyone ready?"

"Yes just turn off the bloody light."

Sally turned off the light. It was by the side of her bed.

"Jenny."

"Yes, Sally."

"Your brother is a really good dancer you now and I …"

"Stop right there what he does is his business I won't help you get a date, I've had enough of that with mates when we were at home."

"You spoil sport."

"Can you two shut up I'm milking in a few hours," Marge said.

The beginning of the year went well for the boys and us girls. We all enjoyed going to the dances. We had become regulars at the local pub in Sutton-on-Derwent. It was much easier for us girls to get back from there; the boys could easily travel from Elvington as they always had the truck.

"Jenny, Jenny."

I could see Lilly running towards me waving her arms in all her flying gear. She looked great.

"Lilly, what are you doing here?"

"Just delivered a Spit up the road and I'm not due back till tomorrow night so if it's alright I thought I would stay the night with you."

"That's great as long as you don't mind topping and tailing with me."

"Well it's been a few years since we did that."

"Ha, ha!"

"Come here let me look at you. It looks like married life suits you."

"Oh yes, Jenny, Thomas is great, if only this war would end and we could be together all the time."

We went in to Pat's and she made Lilly feel welcome like she does with us all. We had some tea then went down to the Crown and met Tim and Peter. It was the first time Lilly had met Peter so I was a bit nervous at first. I wanted them to really get on.

"Tim you look great, and so like my Thomas, but obviously not as good looking."

"Hey we are identical Twins you know."

"Ha-ha!"

"I think you are a little bit biased you know," I said.

We all sat at a small table in the bay window. I introduced Lilly and Peter. The boys went to the bar to get us all some drinks.

"He's really nice, Jenny, you look good together and Tim seems to like him."

"Yes they get on very well but they do have a lot in common."

We chattered all night catching up on all what had been happening in our lives, telling Peter all about our family dynamics. The boys walked us back to Pat's then made their way back to the base.

"Had a good night, Jenny?"

"Yes great thanks, Pat, it was like old times, don't you think, Lilly?"

"It was, and good to meet Peter at last."

"He's a really sensible lad. Don't you think, Lilly?" Pat said.

"He is and they make a great couple."

We had a cup of cocoa with Pat and went to bed. Lilly got up with us girls so she could catch an early train to get back to her base.

We had to get the little barn ready for some of the sheep to be put in as they were showing signs of lambing.

"Just tie the bit of fence to the back of the barn, then we'll put more at the side and front to make separate pens."

"Yes, George, will do."

"Give us a hand, Dolly, just hold it while I tie it."

"I can't wait till we have some lambs."

"You're going to get too attached to them lambs, Dolly," I said.

"No, I know they have to go but it will be good helping with the lambing won't it?"

"Dolly."

"Coming, George."

"Open the barn door and when I open the paddock gate let the sheep in."

"Will do."

"Jenny, you ready in there?"

"Yes, George."

We ushered the sheep into the pens and closed the barn doors.

"Well we're ready for the lambs now girls."

We went in for dinner and discussed how we would put the lambs out with their mums once they had bonded.

"George, George you better come out here," Dolly shouted.

We all made our way to the barn and lo and behold our first lambs had been born.

"Well if they all happen that easy I will be pleased," George said.

We pulled the two lambs round the front of the ewe and she began to clean them.

"The girls will be straight in here when they get back."

"Your Dad would have been so proud of you, George."

"Do you think so, Mam? I took a chance they weren't cheap you know but I wanted to build on what Dad had left me?"

"He would be, lad, he would."

Chapter Seven

Tragedy Comes To Elvington 1943

It was March 11th and we had all just heard the devastating news that there had been casualties at Elvington. Two aircraft had been lost on a raid to Munich. Fortunately for us nobody we knew personally, but Peter, Tim and Roddy knew them and it brought it all too close to home. We were all afraid for the boys and I knew it had unsettled the squadron.

"Peter, I was so scared when I heard about the two planes with you and Tim out on ops."

"Jenny, don't, come here, darling."

"I'm sorry, Peter, I really am, I know this isn't what you want to hear."

"It'll be alright, you'll see, keep your chin up."

"I will, I love you, Peter."

We all pulled together in the village of Sutton-on-Derwent and we tried to forget what was happening over in Elvington. We were well into the lambing by now and having quite a few sets of twins, and one set of triplets. George was really pleased with his sheep and by next year he would have a good flock.

"Well only three left to lamb, Gaynor, then I might get a bit more sleep."

"Good, it's cold in bed without you, I knew I married you for something."

"Cheeky."

All the sheep were in the top paddock with their lambs so that made life a little easier for us.

"Can't wait to get back home tonight and have a bath, I stink after mucking out those pigs."

"How long will it be before Dotty has her litter?"

"Well looking at the size of her the next day or so. That's why George got me to do a complete muck out because you know how funny she gets when she first has her litter."

"Goodness, Dolly, you stink."

"Thanks, Marge, I love you too."

"I'll put your clothes straight to soak, Dolly, you get yourself up in the bath."

"Thanks, Pat."

We all sat down to a real good stew, more veg stew than meat, but really tasty. Then we all went in to the front parlour to listen to the wireless the nine o'clock news came on.

"Can you hear that, Dolly?"

"Yes."

"It's loud tonight, sounds like they're all going out on ops," said Sally.

"I hope they all get back alright."

"I'll never sleep now worrying about Tim and Peter."

"Try not to think about it, Jenny, you need your sleep we're milking in the morning."

We made our way up to bed and I lay their listening for the planes to come back. When they eventually come back I had fallen to sleep and didn't realise one of the bombers was missing shot down over Berlin.

"Bang, bang!"

"Who can that be this early on a morning?"

I ran down the hall my heart was pumping out of my chest I could see the person on the door step was in uniform I opened the door and Peter was standing there with Paul, he looked so solemn. I could feel my stomach starting to churn I knew straight away what it was.

"It's, Tim isn't it? Peter, it's Tim!"

"Yes, my darling, I'm so sorry."

I could feel my legs begin to buckle and I slid to the floor. The next thing I remember I was back in bed with Peter sat with me with Dolly and Paul.

"Jenny, I'm so sorry darling, but I thought I better let you know as officially they will send the telegram to your parents."

I Squealed, "Oh, Mum and Dad, I need to get home, I need to be with them."

"You're in no condition to travel alone and as we are now short I won't get leave."

I began to sob uncontrollably in to my pillow.

"I'll go and let George know what's happened. You stay here and get some rest."

Dolly made her way up to the farm George knew something was wrong as we should have been milking that morning.

"Dolly, you alright what's happened?"

"It's Tim, Jenny's brother; he was shot down over Berlin. She is in a bit of a state. Sorry we didn't make it to milk."

"I knew there was something, you girls are never late."

"She wants to go home. She's worried about her Mum and Dad and there's Tom. It's different when they're twins but she's in no state to travel alone."

"Listen it will take you an age to get a travel warrant. Now I want you to take the truck and take her home. You will be back tomorrow and we will be sure she has got back safe."

"Are you sure, George?"

"Yes he's sure," said Gaynor. "Take this broth with you. They won't feel like cooking or eating much but hopefully it will help."

"Thanks, you two, you are so good to us."

"Get on with you, off you go."

Dolly drove the truck back to Pat's. The boys were still there and Pat was rushing around the kitchen trying to keep busy making tea for everyone. I think she was trying not to think of her Tony, but it brings it all too close when something like this happens.

Dolly explained to all of us what George had said and I began to sob all over again.

"You get your stuff ready, Dolly, and I'll help Jenny to dress," Pat said.

I was so quiet I just sat at the side of Dolly in the truck.

"Bye, darling, I will try and get some leave to come and get you, Jenny. Jenny?"

"Sorry, Peter, yes I will ring the base."

Dolly drove to Wakefield I just sat in the truck. Dolly tried to talk to me but I just stared out of the window.

"Jenny, Jenny."

"Sorry, Dolly."

"We're here you go in and I'll get your bag."

Dolly waited outside for a while not wanting to intrude knowing the emotion that would be behind that door. I opened the door and went down the dark passage Mum was at the stove and Dad was in his chair. They wouldn't have had the telegram yet. I was glad I was here to tell them but also screaming inside with the pain that I would be causing them.

"Jenny, love, why didn't you write and tell us you were coming?"

"Jenny, are you alright?" Dad said.

"Sit down, Mum, I have something to tell you."

"It's Tim, isn't it, no, no don't tell me I don't want to know."

"Mum."

"No, no!"

"Ann, sit down, love."

"I've got dinner to do."

"No, love, come here."

Mum fell to her knees and Dad ran to her and helped her into a chair, Dolly came in and introduced herself and went to make us all a cup of tea.

"Jenny, tell me what happened to my son."

"No, Bill!"

"Ann we need to know."

Dolly told them what happened to Tim's bomber, about being shot down over Berlin and how Peter came round with Paul to tell Jenny.

"We need to get in touch with Thomas and Lilly."

"I'll sort that out today for you before I go back tomorrow."

"Thanks Dolly that will be a great help."

Within twenty four hours Thomas and Lilly were at home with the family and Dolly had gone back to Sutton-on-Derwent.

Thomas what will happen to Tim's things now?"

"They will send you all he had on base."

The telegram had now arrived and Mum just kept saying, "He could be alive they say he is only missing, only missing."

"They have to say that Mum because they haven't got a body."

"Thomas!"

"Mum we have to except Tim has gone. It won't help you to keep believing he's coming back."

"You have become so hard, Thomas, since you went away."

"I have no choice with what we go through up there in the sky."

"Sorry, Tom, take no notice of me."

"It's alright, Mum, I now it's hard for you especially when I'm still flying."

There was a knock on the door. Lilly went to see who it was.

"Peter it's so good to see you come on in."

Peter came through to the kitchen and I threw my arms around his neck. We just stood together. Just to be in his arms made me feel better.

"Mr and Mrs Reed. I wish we could have met in better circumstances."

"It's alright lad, you're welcome anytime. How much leave you got?"

"Only twenty four hours, I thought I would come and take Jenny back then she wouldn't be traveling alone. I borrowed a mate's car."

"Tom, this is Peter my boyfriend, and he was a good friend of Tim's."

"Hello, Tom, I can't believe how much you are like Tim. It's like he's still here."

"I know they were even more alike when they were boys," Mum said.

We spent most of the day together, Peter then stayed on the sofa. When I went downstairs for a drink I sat on the edge of the sofa and looked at Peter sleeping soundly. I stroked his dark hair. I brought the blankets up and round his neck. Could I go through this risk losing Peter like Tim? No, but I couldn't leave him either. Peter was my world I loved him with all my heart. The next day Peter and I said our goodbyes.

"Mum, take care, try not to worry about our Thomas."

"I will try, my girl, look after my baby, Peter, and yourself."

"Will do, Mrs Reed."

"Ann, call me Ann."

We made our way back to Sutton-on-Derwent and as we travelled along the quiet country roads. I looked out of the window. It was the beginning of April and the birds were singing. It was a lovely spring day. The world was carrying on. Nothing had changed but my big brother had gone forever.

"Jenny, I know this is probably the wrong time, but because of what has happened to Tim it has made me look at my life in a different way."

"What?"

"I'm doing this all wrong I know."

"Peter, just say what you mean. One thing since Tim – we need to say exactly what we mean."

"That's what I mean, I want us to be married as soon as we can, I want us to have at least some time together, before anything happens. I know I'm being selfish but I love you and I want to be with you for as long as possible."

"You're not being selfish, darling, I have been thinking the same thing on the journey home. I would love to be married to you and I think Mum and Dad would understand that."

"Still I will write to your father and ask him for your hand."

"Tim would have loved it. He really did like you."

"I really liked him too."

Chapter Eight

Jenny and Peter /May 1943

"Hi Jenny it's good to have you back, just take your time today and settle yourself back in. You've had a big shock."

"Thanks, George, and for letting Dolly take me home, it made a big difference to Mum and Dad being with them."

"Good I'm glad."

Milking was done and the cows fed then we made our way back to the house for breakfast.

"Missed this, Gaynor, your breakfasts are a legend."

"Getaway with you, Jenny, You girls make it worthwhile, especially the way Dolly puts it away."

"Ha, ha, ha."

"I've got something to tell you all. Well, Peter has asked me to marry him."

"Jenny, why didn't you tell me at home?"

"Well I didn't know how you would all react so soon after Tim; I don't want you to think we are being selfish."

"Jenny we can understand why, especially after what happened to Tim. We will do everything we can for you both."

"Thanks, Gaynor that does make things easier."

"As long as you don't go having any babies I don't want to lose one of my girls."

"George."

"Well I could be sent anyone."

"Ha, ha, ha."

We all finished our breakfast. I felt much better about everything with the support of Dolly and the Bakers. I will tell Pat and the boys tonight. Peter and I had both written to Mum and Dad and I have written to Thomas and Lilly and we're waiting to hear back from them all. At supper I told Pat and she was true to form and made me feel even better about the wedding.

"Have you got a date yet, Jenny?"

"No, but Peter has phoned the Vicar at that lovely little church in Sutton-on-Derwent St Michaels and were going round there tonight."

"What you going to wear?" Sally asked.

"Well I hadn't really thought about it with it being so quick."

"You'll struggle, there's not much about, I have been looking for weeks for when Paul and I get wed at Christmas," Marge said.

"As long as I get married to Peter I don't care what I wear."

"No but your Mum and Dad will. You're their only daughter and it would help to make it special after what happened to Tim."

"Never thought of that, Pat."

Pat left the room and we all sat round the range. It had been a cold day for April.

"Do you want cocoa, Dolly?"

"Yes please."

"How about you, Philip?"

"No thanks."

"Jenny, I'll have one."

I heard Pat shouting as she came back down the stairs. She came into the kitchen with a large box and Pat put it on the table.

"What's that, Mum?" Philip said.

"Well this is something I thought would never be worn again. I only had boys. It's my wedding dress. I would be so pleased if you would wear it. You girls have become a part of my family. It's like having four new daughters at home."

"Pat, are you sure?"

"Yes."

"Well I won't want to wear it," Philip said.

We all laughed.

"Go upstairs to your brother, Philip."

"Alright, Mam I will."

"Well let's see if it fits, Jenny."

"Pat oh Pat, how lovely, you must have looked wonderful."

Pat went in to the parlour and brought back a photo of her and John on their wedding day.

"John's Mum made it. She was a dress maker I was the envy of all my friends."

We took the dress out, Pat and the girls helped me try it on.

"Well that fits better than what I thought it would. Just need a little taking in at the waist, the length's alright. The neck sits nice."

"Pat, I love it, I will be so honoured to wear this beautiful dress."

"Dolly's crying."

"What's wrong with you, Dolly?"

"All this wedding talk and seeing you in that dress, I always cry at weddings."

"Ha, ha-ha."

"What are you going to be like when you are stood behind me as my bridesmaid?"

"Me, me?"

"Yes you, and I have asked Lilly to be my matron of honour. I'm going to see if Millie and Jill will be my small bridesmaids."

"Jenny I've never been a bridesmaid before, what will we wear?"

"Well, just a summer dress, you and Lilly don't need to match. I need to organise some bouquets for you all and sort something out for the girls."

"Well you have changed your tune since earlier, Jenny."

"Well what you said earlier, Pat, made sense, I was just going to have Lilly but it feels important to have everyone around me now."

I asked Gaynor if it would be alright before I asked the girls. She was over the moon, Edith said she would take the girls to York and try and find them matching summer dresses, she would enjoy that.

"They need new, but I don't know what we will find for the coupons we have, I'll do my best."

"Thanks Edith."

"Don't be daft it will give me an excuse to take them out for the day."

"Good well I'll ask them this afternoon when we go put the chickens away."

The girls started screaming when they knew their Gran was taking them to York shopping. There was no settling them. I went home to get ready for Peter to collect me to go round to the vicarage. It was getting very exciting.

"Hi, Pat, how are you today?"

"Good thanks, Peter."

"Is she ready?"

"She's changed twice; I've told her it's only the vicar."

"Yes but I want to make the right impression," I said as I entered the room.

"Come on, darling, or we're going to be late and that won't give the right impression."

The vicarage was small but very nice. It smelt of damp. The vicar showed us through the passage. We went into the parlour. He had a small fire in the grate. It was very cosy. We sat on a small settee and he sat in a chair by the fire.

"Now then, Peter, isn't it?"

"Yes, sir, and this is Jennifer."

"Yes, but they all call me Jenny."

"Well Jenny it will be then. Have you a date in mind?"

"Well not to be too cheeky but as soon as possible please."

"Well I understand from what Peter said on the phone you have recently lost your brother, Jenny."

"Yes sadly, and it's made us want to do things sooner than we probably would. We still would have wanted to get married though."

"I can understand that. As long as it wasn't the only reason you wanted to marry."

"No, no we love each other."

"Well then let's see when I can fit you in."

He opened his diary. I felt butterflies' in my stomach.

"Well I can fit you in on the first of June but if that's too soon."

"No, no that's fine."

"First of June it is then."

We walked back to Pat's and I told Peter about the dress and about the girls.

"I talked to my Mum and Dad today. They are thrilled and can't wait to meet you. I'll write and tell them the date. We'll have to sort out where both families will stay, darling."

"George says he can put a couple up. I was going to ask Pat about Mum and Dad as I will be leaving from there."

"That would be great and my Mum and Dad could stay at the farm. We've only got Lilly and Thomas to sort out. My brother won't get back of course but I have written to let him know."

"It seems so real now. We've only got three weeks so we better get a move on."

We stood at Pat's front door and Peter took me in his arms. I could feel his heart beating under his uniform. He lifted up my head. I looked in to his eyes; he slowly placed his lips on mine, so soft and warm. He held me in his arms, as he parted from me I felt butterflies in the pit of my stomach. I watched as Peter walked back down the street. I turned and went indoors. I was so happy, I was marrying Peter and I couldn't wait till the first of June.

It was my wedding day, Mum and Dad had arrived last night. Mum and Pat got on straight away. I knew they would. Mum loved the dress and was very thankful to Pat for lending it to me. Thomas and Lilly arrived last night but they stayed at the local pub. They were coming over to Pat's this morning. I opened the curtains all the girls were at work this morning but would be back by lunch time.

"Morning darling have you slept well?"

"Yes thanks, Dad, you?"

"Yes its lovely here, no wonder you feel at home here and Pat is a lovely woman."

"Where is she, Dad?"

"At the Village Hall with your mother, organising the food. I thought I would stay here and organise your breakfast."

"You mean keep out of the women's way."

"You're right there, girl."

There was a knock at the door. It was Thomas and Lilly.

"Lilly, Thomas come in. You both look well."

"Hi, sis are you alright?"

"Yes thanks nervous but alright."

I had some breakfast and Lilly and I went upstairs to sort things out. Dolly got back. Jill and Millie were with her. All excited with their two new dresses that Edith had bought for them. Mum came back with Pat and everything started to happen. Mum and Pat sorted out the girls. Dolly and Lilly got ready with their lovely dresses Dolly was in pink and Lilly was in lilac. The girls were in pale lemon the colours looked great together, very summery. When they were all ready, all our hair done they helped me into my dress. Mum started to cry.

"Mum, don't cry."

"Jenny, you look so beautiful, I can't thank you enough, Pat, she really looks lovely."

"It's nice to know it's been used again, especially with all the work John's mother put into it."

"You lot ready? We need to get Mother and all the girls to the Church."

"Yes."

We all said at the same time. I waited till Thomas and all the others had gone, and then went downstairs. Dad was stood by the door, waiting for Thomas to come back with the car.

"Jenny, oh, Jenny, you look so like your Mum. You are so beautiful, darling."

"Thanks, Dad."

The car horn went. It was Thomas back with the car.

"We better be off Thomas is here."

Neighbours were all outside clapping as we got into the car.

"You look good, sis, that's from me and Tim. He would have been so proud of you today as I am."

Peter and his family were already at the church. My stomach was doing summersaults. I was so nervous. I had not had chance to meet them before as they hadn't arrived until late last night.

The organ began to play.

"You ready, love?" Dad asked.

"As I'll ever be."

I walked down the aisle on Dad's arm; Peter turned round to us and smiled at me. All my nerves had gone and as Dad handed my hand to Peter he looked so proud. The ceremony was quickly over. We made our way to the Hall. Everyone shook our hands as they came through the door. I eventually met Peter's parents.

"It's so good to meet you at last, Mr and Mrs Shepard, but very strange meeting you for the first time at our wedding."

"Yes but we understand why you wanted to get married so soon. We are very pleased; call us Mum and Dad. We have always wanted a daughter, and now we have a beautiful one."

"Here, here." Peter's Dad shouted.

We had a wonderful day. It was all too soon over. We were going to Bridlington for four days honeymoon. We caught the train to York then to Bridlington.

"Well, Mrs Shepard, how does it feel to be an old married woman?"

"Less of the old."

We stayed in a bed and breakfast near the front. It was painted a lovely shade of blue. The elderly lady was proud of her little bed and breakfast. She kept it so neat and tidy. She showed us to her best room and handed Peter the key.

"I hope you like it?"

"Thank you it's lovely."

She closed the door. Peter put the key on the chest of drawers.

"You can see the beach from the window."

"It's a shame about the barb wire on the beach. I suppose these are the things we have to put up with in war time."

"Would you like to go for a walk along the front before dinner?"

"I would love to. I'll just wash up first."

We enjoyed our walk along the front but I was ready for dinner when we got back. Ellie, the land lady, had made us a meal because everything was shut by the time we had arrived. The rest of the four days we would have to eat out.

"Are you ready to go up, darling?"

"I am, but I do feel a little nervous."

"Me too, but don't worry we'll be fine."

We had the most wonderful four days. Being with Peter, made me feel so complete. He is the best thing that ever happened to me. Peter was so patient and gentle and very caring. I loved him more and more. On the journey back home we were on a train packed with service men and women. The train might as well have been empty. Peter and I sat together by the window and only had eyes for each other.

Chapter Nine

Disastrous Raid with Unspeakable Ending

It was straight back to normal when we returned. Peter was straight in at the deep end in the middle of the battle of the Ruhr. Aircraft went missing on operations and many were killed. I worried all the time and since the wedding I hadn't seen much of Peter, so I threw myself into work.

"You look tired, Jenny."

"I'm not sleeping very well, every time I hear the bombers going out I wait till I hear them coming back."

"You can't go on like that, you will make yourself ill."

"I know but all I think about is Tim, and what could happen to Peter."

"Come here."

I put my head on Dolly's shoulder and the tears flowed and I thought I would never stop.

"Does that feel better?"

"Yes but that doesn't change anything, I need to sleep that's all."

We got on with our jobs Hoeing between the crops, I did stone picking and my back was killing me. By the end of the week I was that tired I fell asleep when my head hit the pillow. It was mid-day when I woke. I quickly dressed and went downstairs.

"Why didn't you wake me, I should have been milking this morning? It's my weekend on."

"It's alright Dolly's gone, she said to leave you as you needed your sleep and she was right. Want something to eat?"

"Sorry, Pat, for being sharp with you. It's just I feel bad for not getting up."

"You're alright."

"Will toast do?"

"I'll do it, Pat, thanks."

Dolly came back and I thanked her, she is a good friend.

"All alright up there?"

"Yes, George agreed with me, Best thing was to let you sleep and said he would see you tomorrow."

"Thanks, Dolly, I owe you one."

We decided to go for a drink at the local pub. Dolly said it might help me sleep and not listen for the bombers coming and going.

"I feel much better for the sleep and drink; you're a real good friend."

We got back to Pat's and she was still up knitting.

"Ha, ha, ha."

"You girls sound better it's good to hear you laugh, Jenny."

"Just what I needed and now I'm shattered."

"Good," Pat said.

We went to bed and I went straight to sleep, I didn't hear the bombers come back and didn't know that there were some missing again and that one of the bombers was Peter's.

"Morning, George, lovely morning."

"Yes it is. Good to have you back to normal."

"I think I just needed a good night sleep."

I got on with the milking and washing down the pens. Unbeknownst to me Peter's plane still hadn't come back.

"We'll feed the sheep before breakfast, Jenny, and then we can sort fields out a bit more."

"Alright, George, will do."

Back down at Elvington, Paul was watching out for any aircraft to return back to base.

"Sir, sir there's one coming in."

The plane was smoking from the back and had only two of the four engines working.

"It's not got its gear down, Sir."

"Sound the alarm Action stations; Get the ground crew out?"

"Will do, Sir."

Everybody gathered on the ground they all held their breath as Peter tried to land. The back rudder and gun position was missing it was going to be hard to land.

"Come on, Pete keep it steady."

Boom!

The plane landed and immediately burst in to flames. All the ground crew and all the other crews ran towards the plane. Three got out and there was another explosion at the cockpit, they filled it with foam and Peter was dragged out barely alive. He was suffering from severe burns, they quickly put him in the ambulance and Paul jumped in the back.

"Jenny, my Jenny!"

"Don't worry old man, I will go and see Jenny."

He jumped out of the ambulance and it rushed across the runway towards York.

"Philips, you know Shepherd's wife?"

"Yes sir! She billets with my fiancée."

"Well, you better go and get her straight to the hospital it doesn't look good. They've only just married haven't they, Philips?"

"Yes, Sir."

We were sitting at Gaynor's large kitchen table enjoying a mug of hot tea after a wonderful breakfast. We were discussing the jobs of the day when there was a knock at the door.

"Who could that be this early on a morning?" asked Gaynor.

She got up and went to the door.

"Hello can I help?"

"My name's Paul, I'm from the airfield."

"Oh no, it's Peter isn't it?"

"I'm afraid so."

"You better come in."

"Paul, what you doing here? Peter!" I screamed.

I tried to stand but fell back in to my seat; I suddenly felt nauseous and was sick all over the floor.

"Is he dead?"

"Not when I saw him last, But he's very badly burned the C.O gave me his car to collect you."

I felt the biliousness creeping up again and ran for the door.

"Sorry Gaynor."

"Don't worry I'll sort it you go with Paul and we'll be in touch later today."

"Thanks."

"Come on, Jenny, we better be off. We have to drive to York."

We made the journey in silence most of the way. All sorts of thoughts were going around my head, and then I remembered Peter's parents.

"Paul, what about Peter's parents?"

"Don't worry, the C.O is on that."

"The other boys, how are they?"

"All the crew that were on the plane survived with minor injuries. Thanks' to Peter's skilled piloting."

"All that was on the plane? What does that mean?"

"Well, Roddy was shot straight of his gun turret and the back rudder was gone, two engines and the landing gear didn't come down."

"Oh no poor Roddy."

We spent the rest of the time in silence. It seemed an age before we arrived at the hospital.

"Hello, this is Mrs Shepherd; her husband has just been brought in from Elvington."

"Yes, he's just gone straight to theatre to stabilise him and to dress his burns. You can wait over there I'll organise some tea for you both."

"Thank you."

We waited a number of hours, and then a tall man came across to me and held out his hand.

"Hello, Mrs Shepherd, I'm your husband's doctor, Dr Lewis."

I shook his hand, He sat down beside me.

"Well, Mrs Shepherd."

"Jenny, please call me Jenny. I'm not quite use to the Mrs Shepherd just yet, only been married three weeks."

"Alright, Jenny it is. Peter is stable, we have done what we can to make him comfortable."

"How bad is he, doctor?"

"Not good he has lost his left eye and there is burning to the left side, broken right leg and bad burn's to his right hand, His face is my biggest concern, you will not see much as he is heavily bandaged. It's going to be a long road to recovery; Peter will need you to be strong, especially when the bandages come off. I have seen families never come back after seeing them and then the patient suffers very badly."

"Don't worry, doctor. Just to have my Peter alive is good enough for me."

"Well that's good to hear, I'll take you through now, but don't stay long, he is heavily sedated and you will need rest as much as him."

We went into a side room, you could smell the smell of burned flesh; I felt bilious again but held it back.

"Peter, my darling Peter."

I walked towards the bed, His left hand was the only thing not bandaged I put my hand on top of his. I daren't pick it up in case it hurt him. He had a cage over his burnt leg and his left leg was potted below the knee, a nurse pulled a chair over for me to sit on, I smiled at her, the door was suddenly pushed open. It was Peter's parents. I jumped up and Janet ran to me.

"Jenny, darling, you poor girl, Peter my boy."

Janet stared at Peter, I told her and Bert what had happened and what the doctor had said. She listened to all I told her only holding out a hand for Bert's support she was more concerned for me. She was so strong.

"How did you get here so quickly, Bert?"

"The C.O rang and we closed the garage and got straight in the car. One good thing the roads were empty."

"I'm so glad that you are here."

Janet and Bert went to the local pub and booked themselves in for a few days. Peter was stable, the doctor told us as he was young and fit, he would recover but it would be hard; we were all so grateful for him being spared. I went with

Janet and Bert, they dropped me off at Pat's. We arranged to go to the hospital together the next day.

"Take care, my dear. I will write and tell Peter's brother."

"Thank you, I will let my family know."

"Don't worry, Jenny, we will get through this. He is made of strong stuff that lad of ours."

"Thanks, Bert."

I went into Pat's. Paul had called on his way back to base. The girls were all sat around the table. They all got up and came and put their arms around me. We hugged each other and I shed more tears. I felt easier with Pat and the Girls. I had to be strong with Peter's parents. George came with Gaynor and assured me my job was safe. He had been in touch with the WLA (Women's Land Army) and organised two weeks compassionate leave.

"Thanks, George, you're an angel."

"Don't worry about anything. We will be here for you if you need anything."

"Thanks, Gaynor."

By the time I went to bed I was exhausted. After a few minutes I was fast asleep. I had lots to do the next morning. Pat got me up and made my breakfast, I wrote my letters to the family and helped Pat clean up the breakfast pots.

"You alright, Jenny, you do look very peeky?"

Just as she said this I felt a little dizzy. Pat steered me into a chair.

"You will have to rest and take things easy as much as you can, your body has had a big shock."

A knock came at the door and it was Bert and Janet.

"Come in, come in its good to see you again, sorry it's not better circumstances."

"Thank you, Pat, how's our girl?"

"She's putting on a brave face. She was a little wobbly this morning, so keep an eye on her for me, and make sure she eats something."

"We will, it goes without saying."

I came back into the room.

"Hello, I'm about ready. I'll just get my cardigan."

We made our way to the hospital. Bert said they were staying for a few more days but would have to get back to the garage. They would wait till Peter was a little more stable though. We spent the next two days by Peter's bed then on the third day the day Peter's parents were due to leave, the Doctor came over to us as he saw us coming down the corridor.

"Hello, Jenny, how are you coping?"

"Well, thank you, Doctor."

"We've stopped the induced sleep to let Peter come round and I'm glad to say he is conscious. He's ready to see you all."

We went through the door. Peter was sat up with pillows behind him, as soon as he heard our voices he shouted out.

"Jenny, Jenny is that you!"

"Yes darling I'm here and your Mum and Dad."

I rushed to the bed. Peter held out his good hand I grabbed it with both mine and began to kiss it tenderly.

"Peter, my darling, it's so good to hear your voice."

"Mum?"

Janet begins to cry Bert held Janet in his arms.

"Come on, love, the lad doesn't want to hear this."

"I'm sorry I really am. I tried not to crash the old girl."

"You did fantastic you saved all those boys lives."

"Not Roddy, though, not Roddy."

"Peter you couldn't do anything about Roddy. The boys say he wouldn't have felt anything. It was instant."

"I know, but it doesn't make it any easier. I'll just look like a monster, I should have died with Roddy."

"Peter, please don't, we will get through this together."

"You don't have to; if it's too much for you I don't want you to waste your life with a freak."

"Peter, don't you dare do this to that girl. She has been sat by your side ever since this happened to you. I don't think she would be here if she didn't love you, son!" Bert shouted.

Peter began to cry. I held him near to me.

"I love you, Peter, for better for worse. Have you forgotten already, you are my wonderful husband?"

"Sorry, I am truly sorry, darling, Mum and Dad."

"Good, then I don't want any reports from Jenny that you are feeling sorry for yourself. We know it will be hard and a long road but we'll get there."

The two weeks were soon over and I was back to work. Peter was getting ready for his pot to come off and had been reviewed by the Doctor for his first operation on his hand and face. I made my way to the farm with Dolly. It was strange walking back up the lane.

"It's great to have you back Jenny. It's been so busy without you."

"Glad to be back. It will be good to have something to occupy my mind, Peter's having his pot off today and they're assessing him for facial surgery and the grafts on his hand."

"How's he feeling now?"

"Well since his parents had that bit of a chat to him he doesn't feel sorry for himself. But he hasn't seen himself without the bandages yet."

"Morning girls."

"Morning," we both said together.

"After breakfast I would like you two to go over the tractor and check her out. We need her in tip top condition before we start to get the crops in."

"Will do."

We checked her over and she was all ready to go just like us.

Chapter Ten

Life Goes On /1943-1944

We settled in to Peter having operations and skin grafts. He became quite grumpy after each operation. He was keen to get the bandages off each time. He had grafts to his hand and had most of the movement back as it wasn't as tight now. He could open and close it with some considerable concentration he was down to have the final operation on his face after Christmas. Marge and Paul were getting ready for their wedding on Christmas Eve. They were getting married at the same church as Peter and I.

"Everything sorted, Marge?"

"Oh I do hope so, we've been organising it for long enough."

Marge was leaving the land army when she got married. She had found a lovely little cottage to rent in the village. She wanted to start a family straightway. She was a bit older than the rest of us. The build-up to the wedding at Pat's house brought great excitement. I was waiting for a letter to come from Lilly. I had written to see if she had leave at Christmas, to see if she could come spend it with me. I knew Peter could do with some cheering up as he waited for his final operation.

"Hello, Jenny, don't usually see you here at this time of day. Got the morning off to go see Peter?"

"Yes to discuss his last operation after Christmas. I'm expecting a letter from Lilly."

"Well there's a few here for you girls, and it looks like one from Tony for Pat."

"She'll be pleased. She hasn't heard from him in ages. He's terrible at writing and visiting."

"Boys, he always was a tearaway as a kid."

"Well I better go. See you later, Beryl."

"Bye, Jenny."

I went inside and put all the girl's post on the hall table then took mine and Pat's into the kitchen. Pat was washing the breakfast dishes.

"Got your letter then I see?"

"Yes and one for you from Tony," Beryl said.

"Well she would know. She recognises all the different people's writing in the village."

"Great, Lilly can come for Christmas. Hopefully Thomas, too, that will cheer Peter up. What does Tony have to say?"

"I don't believe it, he's got a whole week's leave at Christmas and he's coming home. It will be the first time since he went away that I'll have all my boys together."

"Oh, Pat, that's great news, a house full for Christmas, hope we'll all fit in."

"Course we will. It's always better when the house is full at Christmas. Then there is the wedding on Christmas Eve."

"At least Marge and Paul have their house to go back to after the wedding."

"Well I better be off, I have to be at the hospital by two to see the Doctor. See you later, Pat."

"Good luck, give my love to Peter."

"I will."

I made my way to the hospital and was met at the door to Peter's room by the Doctor.

"Hello, Doctor."

"Hello, Jenny, shall we go in?"

"Peter, darling, you're out of bed?"

"Yes and I have been to the door. It's so good to be back on my feet."

"Well that's enough excitement for one day, Peter. Let's talk about the operation. You know that this will be it, whichever way it goes."

"We do," I said.

"Well I'm pretty confident; your skin is very good at healing. The false eye will give you a much more natural look. So how do you feel?"

"Nervous. Knowing that this is it; it won't get any better. I have seen some of the lads, though, that have come out of the spits, and I'm very lucky."

"Well that's the right attitude. I'll let you two have some time together before Jenny has to get back."

"Thank you, Doctor, for everything," I said.

"Oh, darling, you look really well and to see you standing – it's amazing. Guess what? Lilly is coming for Christmas and hopefully Thomas too. Pat had a letter from Tony. He's got a week's leave and will be coming home for Christmas."

"Bet Pat's over the moon?"

"She is. Then there's Paul and Marge's wedding. Then to top it off – your operation after Christmas."

"Six months ago we were getting ready for our wedding at the same church."

"I don't know where the last six months has gone."

"Well for me it's been in here."

"I know, darling, but we're nearly there now. We will have our time, I'm hoping that when you go to the convalescence home in Scarborough I'll get some leave, then we can spend some time together."

"That sounds good, just to lie beside you and hold your beautiful body will be worth waiting for."

"Peter."

I made my way back to Pat's, the thought of what Peter had said remained in my mind. It would be worth waiting for, we hadn't been together in that way since our honeymoon. It would be so good to be together again. Christmas had sneaked up on us all quite quickly. The weather had taken a turn for the worse. It had been frosty for days then the day before Christmas Eve we had a blanket of snow covering the village and surrounding area.

"Won't the church look romantic covered in the snow, Marge? Are you glad?"

"Oh yes, I have always wanted a white wedding at Christmas."

"Hope Tony gets here soon, he should have been here at dinner time," Pat said.

"It'll be the snow, the trains are bad enough when the weather's good."

"Philip bank that fire up won't you? At least we can have it warm in here for when he gets home."

"I will, Mam."

"I'll put the kettle on, Pat. You sit down for a bit. He won't get back any sooner if you run round the kitchen."

"Gosh it's cold out there, Mam, and you never guess what I found out there."

"Hi, Mam."

"Tony come here. Where have you been, I was so worried about you?"

"Give me a minute let me get in."

We all sat round Pat's table and tucked in to a lovely stew, and it actually had meat in it. Philip had caught a couple of rabbits in his brother's honour. Pat was glowing and couldn't stop looking at her boys; it was nice to see Pat happy.

"Well what do you think of him, Dolly?"

"Tony, he's alright, I've met him before, you were on leave the last time he was home."

"He's very handsome. I hope he goes to the dance."

"He's a bit of a lad you know, everyone says so."

"I always was attracted to the bad boys."

"Sally, I always thought you were quiet."

"They do say the quietest are the worst."

The next day was totally taken up with Marge and Paul's wedding. It was great, very cold but great. Marge got her wish, a white wedding. They went back to their cottage to spend Christmas day together. Dolly and I were up early for milking and couldn't believe this was our third Christmas at the farm. The girls were running round and to hear them enjoy themselves was great. Presents were thin on the ground, food too, but being in the country we did stand a better chance than in the city. After milking we went up to the house for our usual big breakfast. The girls were in the parlour with their grandma learning to knit. Dolly and I had our meal with George and Gaynor.

"How did the wedding go yesterday, girls?"

"She looked lovely and got her wish for a white wedding. They're tucked up at their cottage together now."

"Bet Pat's enjoying having Tony at home?"

"She is. So is Sally."

"Sally."

"Yes she has fallen for him in a big way."

We finished our breakfast then bedded up the stock and fed all the cows.

"Well there we go another Christmas morning shift out of the way. You ready."

"Yes."

"I'll tell George were done and will see him tomorrow."

"Alright, Dolly."

"Are you going to get to see Peter today with there being no transport?"

"Peter's parents are coming this afternoon to take me up in the car."

"That's great. Are you going to the dance mid-week?"

"Well I would but I'm going up to stay in a b and b to see Peter through his operation, so I better put the work in before then."

"I'll go and keep an eye on Sally and Tony. He's getting as bad as her the way they were last night at dinner. It was getting that bad even Pat will begin to notice."

"Well sooner you than me."

Christmas dinner was good we all ate well. Tony got his Mam a lovely paste broach and Pat was proudly wearing it and seemed oblivious to Tony and Sally flirting with each other all day.

"That's a beautiful broach, Pat, you must love it?"

"I do and Mark and Philip got me a new head scarf I have the best boys."

"What time are Peter's parents coming, Jenny?"

"At about four thirty, I think we can visit at six till eight as its Christmas day. They're bringing me back before going back to Blackburn tonight."

74

Peter's parents came and we made our way to the hospital in York. We spent a lovely couple of ours together. He seemed quite cheerful and very chatty which was a good sign.

"They've given me a date for the operation 3rd January."

"Good I'll have to sort my leave out."

"We will be thinking of you, son. Don't worry you have done great so far."

I hoped they were right but they didn't see him straight after the grafts and the mood swings he went through. Well I'll have to wait and see. They drove me back to Pat's and we said our good byes.

"Let us know how he goes dear. We will be thinking of you both."

"I will, drive carefully Bert with this snow."

"I will."

They drove away and I went into Pat's.

The next few days went quickly as Pat was enjoying spending time with Tony. Tony took Pat out to the pictures and out for a meal at the local cafe but on the night of the dance he told Pat he was going to the dance as he owed it to all the single girls. We all knew he was going to be with Sally. He was always a jack the lad but always knew what he wanted. Like when he joined the air force. It was quite a shock to see Tony all flushed whenever Sally was around. The casual flirting had turned to more serious cosy chats. Then on the evening of the dance. The girls made their way to the village hall.

"I'll catch up, Dolly, just putting my coat in the cloak room."

"All right, I'm keeping mine on I'm freezing."

"Sally, Sally."

"Tony, are you all right?"

"Yes but I want to talk to you."

"Let's go sit down, Dolly's getting some seats."

"No I want to take you out of here. I need to talk to you."

"What about, Dolly?"

"She'll be alright, please Sally."

"Alright."

They walked into the village then went in to the local pub. Tony sat Sally at a little table in the window and went to the bar. Dolly was passing up and down the hall wondering where Sally and Tony had got to.

"I'll kill her when I see her. I can guess where they are."

Dolly had had enough and went back to Pat's. Pat was sat by the range keeping warm.

"Hello love you alright?"

Dolly didn't want to cause any trouble for Sally and Tony so she kept quiet.

"I've got a migraine so I thought I wouldn't spoil the others night."

"I'll make you a cuppa and you can get yourself to bed. Jenny's already gone up."

"Thanks, Pat."

"What you doing back so early?"

"Sorry, Jenny, did I wake you?"

"No can't get to sleep for thinking about Peter's operation."

"Sally and Tony gave me the slip; I told Pat I had a migraine."

"Well they're both of age and there's nothing we can do now."

"As long as Pat doesn't get hurt in all this I don't care."

Pat had a tearful goodbye, on New Year's Eve, Sally was very quiet. Sat at the table we all had tea the mood was very solemn.

"It's quiet tonight with no Marge and now Tony's gone."

"I know. I do hope this is the last New Year of the war," I said.

We were all seeing the New Year in at home as we were all working early in the morning. Mark and Philip stayed up to see the New Year in with us all.

"Philip, go outside and get a piece of coal. We will shout to let you know when to come back and bring in nineteen forty four."

"All right, Mam."

"Five, Four, Three, Two, One Happy New Year. Come in, Philip."

We all hugged and kissed wishing each other Happy New Year.

Chapter Eleven

Life Changing News for Jenny /July 1944

I made my way to the train station and to my platform I felt like I was in a dream everything was just passing me by. I boarded the train I was watching the rain running down the windows, all the snow was turning to slush. I was apprehensive of what mood Peter would be in when I went to visit him tonight. I arrived in York and made my way to the bed and breakfast. It was a lovely little place and a young woman answered the door, she was covered in flour.

"Hello, can I help?"

"Yes I phoned about a room for a few days."

"Oh yes, Mrs Shepard, Come on in I'm Sarah."

She showed me to a small but cosy lounge and I signed the register, Sarah asked me if I wanted a tea.

"That would be lovey thanks."

"Come through to the kitchen and get warm by the range."

"Something smells nice."

"Thank you, I try to bake at least once a week although the ingredients are hard to sort after."

"Well it smells good."

"What's the reason for your visit, Mrs Shepard, if you don't mind me asking?"

"Jenny you can call me, Jenny. My husband was a bomber pilot and the plane exploded on landing and he was badly burnt. He's having his last operation tomorrow."

"I'm very sorry to hear that, Jenny, I hope it goes well."

"Thank you."

Sarah showed me to the top of the house and a little room in the eves.

"Hope this will be all right for you, it's small but it's very cosy."

"It's very nice. Thank you."

"I'll leave you to unpack and freshen up and see you when you come down."

"Thanks, Sarah."

I unpacked my small case and freshened up. I felt nervous about going to the hospital but it would be good to see Peter. I came down and said goodbye to Sarah and made my way to the hospital. It got dark early that evening and it was already dusk when I arrived at the hospital.

"Peter you're up and about on your own."

"Yes I thought we would go for a walk round the gardens now it's stopped raining."

"Oh, Peter, that would be wonderful."

We held hands and walked round the small garden of the hospital, all the flower beds were down to vegetables. It was really getting dark now but for the first time in six months I had my Peter back.

"Don't worry about tomorrow, I know I have put you through so much this last few months but I am at peace now with how I look. Tomorrow is just the icing on the cake and being with you is the most important thing in my life."

"Oh Peter you don't know what that means to me, I have been so worried."

Peter drew me to him and held me close it felt so good to be in his arms again.

"I love you, darling, and I can't wait till this bloody war is over and we can spend the rest of our lives together and start a family of our own."

"Me too, Peter darling."

We went back to the main door. It was all too soon time to leave. Peter had to get his rest for tomorrow.

"I'll be here when you wake up tomorrow darling. Good luck."

"Good night, Jenny, see you tomorrow."

I walked back to the bed and breakfast. Sarah welcomed me back through the door.

"It's cold out. You must be freezing come on in the kitchen. Would you like a cocoa to warm you up?"

"Oh yes please, Sarah."

"Is your husband ready for tomorrow?"

"Yes, better than what I thought he was going to be."

I went to sleep more easily than I had thought earlier in the day. I arrived at the hospital and was shown to Peter's room soon after he was brought back. They made him comfortable.

"How did it go, doctor?"

"Very well, Jenny, better than I could have hoped. We will take the bandages off the day after tomorrow. It heals better that way. Will you still be here for that?"

"Oh yes, my boss has been great about me having leave."

"Good, good, I'll see you then. Bye for now."

I held Peter's hand and he was very cold he didn't make any movements till late afternoon when he opened his eyes.

"Hello, Peter darling, it's all over and it went well."

"Jenny."

"Don't try and talk just rest, darling."

I went back to the bed and breakfast and prepared myself for the day the bandages came off. The staff at the hospital had been fantastic with Peter and made me feel at ease.

"Good morning, doctor. Well I'm ready if you are."

"Bring the trolley over nurse. Take a seat, Jenny."

The doctor slowly took off the bandages and went right up to Peter looking close. I couldn't see at that time for the doctor and the nurse. The Doctor took off the gauze and stood back.

"Well I'm very pleased, Peter. How does it feel?"

"It's not nearly as tight as it was but sore. Can I see?"

"Nurse the mirror."

She passed the mirror to Peter and he went silent I thought he was upset but then.

"Doctor you're a genius. A real genius and the eye, well it makes all the difference. I know I won't win any beauty contests but it is great doctor."

"I can't believe it, I have my Peter back."

"Well there's quite a way to go yet, Peter, you will have to be transferred to the convalescence home for probably a month for the healing process to continue."

"Thank you for everything you have done for us both doctor."

I said my good byes to Peter and made my way back to collect my belongings from the bed and breakfast and went to catch my train. The feeling I had of anticipation on my way here had gone. My life had changed over the last few days could it get any better than it felt right now? I had a letter from Lilly to say she was so happy that Peter was on the mend and she hoped to get back to Elvington before much longer and was still happy flying her Spits. I worried about Lilly and Thomas knowing they were flying in the dangerous skies. It was time for Peter to go to Scarborough and I was hoping to get time off to spend with him but we were getting ready for lambing and it was too busy to let me go. I wrote and told Peter who was very upset but he understood. George had been more than generous with my time off. We were off and the lambs were coming thick and fast. Dolly and I stayed at the farm to give George a rest at night as he would have double the sheep lambing this year. It was good to be with the sheep. We took it in turns to be with them, sleeping in-between. It was coming up to a year since Tim had been shot down. I couldn't believe what had happened in just one year Mum would be feeling down and Thomas had spent a year without his twin. I wrote to them both knowing they would be feeling the same way as me. I had the best letter from Peter.

Hello my darling Jenny,

Guess what? I have been discharged from the convalescence home. I'm waiting for my travel warrant I have two weeks leave then I will be back to work, sadly not in the air as my hand isn't good enough but I will be re-trained and hopefully posted back to Elvington behind a desk. Will write back and let you know when I get the travel warrant. Do you think you could ask Pat if I could lodge at hers while I have my leave that way we could be together?
All my love
Your loving husband Peter.

I couldn't believe what I was reading, at last Peter was coming back to me.

"You look pleased with yourself. Good news I presume?"

"Oh, Pat, the best, Peter is being discharged and has two weeks leave before he gets to be re-trained."

"Oh Jenny, that's wonderful news's. Where will he go?"

"Well he's asked me if he could stay here so we could spend some time together. We're much too busy at the farm to have any leave."

"Well we will have to move things round but I think we could sort it all out."

Peter arrived at Pat's and he looked wonderful. It was just wonderful to have him with me.

"Hello Pat thank you for allowing me into your home. You are very kind."

"You two have been through enough so to have you here is a pleasure."

Peter came into Pat's warm kitchen and put down his bag.

"Want a cuppa?"

"Yes please."

"The girls won't be back till around six and we will eat with them if that's alright?"

"That's great, Pat. Is there anything you want me to do?"

"You could get some wood for the fire."

"It will just be good to be able to do normal things."

"What you going to be doing after your leave? Will you be able to fly again?"

"Afraid not but I will end up back at Elvington. Things are going to be changing over there but it's all hush, hush. Walls have ears and all that."

"Well, Jenny, will be pleased about that."

Just then Dolly and I came through the door.

"Jenny will be pleased about what indeed?"

"Jenny, darling, I'll be stationed back at Elvington after training."

"Oh, Peter, that's the best news."

We all gathered around the table and chatted about everything before eating our meal. Then Peter and I washed the pots and chatted about what we were going to do on Peter's leave.

"Come on, Peter, let's take your bags up. Where have you put him, Pat, in with the boys?"

"No I've put your stuff in my room for the two weeks."

"Pat, you can't do that. It's your room."

"I can. It's only for two weeks and you two deserve the time together."

"I can't thank you enough, Pat, you have been really kind to us."

"Get away with ya, Peter, you're the hero around here."

We all laughed, it was going to be a wonderful two weeks. Peter went from strength to strength and we did things we never got to do before. He spent time at the farm with me while I was working and getting the fresh air and food he needed from both Pat and Gaynor whose main aim in life was to feed people. It was all too soon at the end of the two weeks and time for Peter to go back to be re-trained. I would miss him while he was away but at least I would know he would be safe. We got back to normal. The season turned to summer and we were hay making, it was hot and we were tired but it was nice being outside I loved it.

"God it's hot Jenny I think I might melt."

"I know, I hope Gaynor comes with lunch soon I need a sit down and a drink."

"Well, we only need to turn it tomorrow then we can get it in and that will be a job well done."

We worked hard for the rest of the morning in the hot sun. I could see George waving at us at the bottom of the field; we were expecting Gaynor with lunch but as long as we had lunch I didn't care.

"What's George doing?"

"I don't know he seems to be waving at us."

"No. I think he wants us to go down."

"We don't usually go in for lunch when we're in the field."

"Something must be wrong."

We started to walk down the field George was getting frantic and jumping up and down so we began to run as best as we could with our big boots on. He was waving something in the air.

"What's he waving?" I said.

We eventually got down to George and he looked at me. He had a telegram in his hand I knew it couldn't be Peter so I screamed. "Thomas!"

"No, no, it's not bad news. Here read it."

I turned the telegram over and looked at the words on it. I read it and didn't believe what I saw. I read it again.

Jenny – Tim has been found – he is in a prison of war camp. He had lost his memory – but now got it back – will write with more details, Mum. Tears had filled my eyes and Dolly was shouting.

"What did it say?"

I just couldn't speak and handed the telegram over to her. After a few minutes she wrapped her arms around me and we jumped up and down. I was stunned I couldn't think of what to say.

"Come on, you two, we will have dinner at the farm, I don't think Jenny's going to be much use to use the rest of the day."

George sent me home and I felt like I was on air.

"Jenny, what you doing here?"

I gave Pat the telegram and she looked at me with a solemn face she then read the words of the telegram.

"Jenny, oh Jenny!" Pat screamed. "Oh I am so pleased for you."

"Mum must have sent it straight up to the farm knowing I would be there till late, I just couldn't believe it."

I got a letter from Mum two days later with all the details on Tim.

Dear Jenny

Good news' wasn't it? Well Tim crashed landed over Berlin and him and two other crew survived. He had head injuries but the other two were unhurt and sent straight to a prison of war camp. Tim was unconscious for some time and had memory loss and they didn't know who he was till last month and then when his memory began to come back the Red Cross let his squadron know and then they sent us a telegram. Dad said not to get too excited as he will be at a prison of war camp once he is better, but I said I didn't care as at the moment, my Timmy was alive. Thomas and Lilly are also over the moon as you can imagine. We will have to wait till he is sent to a camp but the Red Cross will let us know where we can write to. I can't tell you how good it feels just to talk about him in the now and not in the past.

Will write soon all my love Mum.

The news was fantastic but I couldn't understand Dad, he was always the more optimistic of the two, I wrote and told Peter and he was so shocked but elated. He had nearly finished at the training camp and was delighted not to be going behind a desk; he'd been trained with the wireless ops and would be with Paul in the tower. The 77 squadron had moved to the newly opened full Sutton airport. In May 1944 Elvington had then become host to two French squadrons. The base still had English running the tower and the ground crew and nothing else had changed. Soon after the 77 squadron had left, troops were being moved all over Britain. As we now know it was the build-up to D-Day; massive army convoys the sight that something big was happening. Then came the great announcement and we all prayed for success. On the sixth of June 1944 D-Day took place. We all hoped the war would be over before Christmas. Not much changed except the normal bombing raids were a thing of the past. Hitler had now given us the V1 and V2 over the south of the country. The troops were making progress, slowly things were going in the right direction. Meanwhile Peter eventually joined Paul in the tower at Elvington and was very happy.

"Morning, Sally, you're up early."

"Yes I couldn't sleep."

"You're not in today are you?"

"It's my Saturday off."

"You don't look well, Sally. You all right?"

"Yes fine."

I walked towards the kitchen stove to put the kettle on and all of a sudden.

"Sally."

Sally was on the floor I ran over to her and tried to get her up. I couldn't I then opened her dressing gown to loosen her clothing to see if that would help I got the shock of my life Sally was heavily pregnant and had been hiding it.

"Pat, Pat, I need your help, come quickly."

I heard Pat coming down the stairs.

"What's wrong, Jenny? Oh my God, she's pregnant; let's get her on the sofa. Careful."

"Phillip!"

Pat got Phillip to go fetch the doctor. They were back within minutes by now Sally had begun to come round.

"Sally are you all right? Why didn't you tell us?"

Sally began to cry then the doctor asked us all to leave the room. Thirty minutes later, the doctor called us all in.

"Well doctor how is she?"

"Well, Sally, is it all right, can I tell them?"

"Yes, please do," Sally said with tears rolling down her face.

"Sally is, as you can see, pregnant. About seven months she said. It was Christmas when her and the baby's father were together and she was afraid to tell as she knew she would be sent away out of the land army."

"But why didn't you tell us?" said Pat.

More tears came from Sally and I said, "It's Tony's isn't it Sally?"

"Yes!" she cried.

"What, my Tony, not my Tony!" Pat said astonished.

"I'm sorry, Pat, I let you down please don't hate me."

There was silence in the room that seemed forever, and then Pat said, "Come here, you silly girl. I should have seen this, what with how you two were at Christmas. Does he know?"

"No, I was too scared to tell him."

"Well we better get that sorted and the land army."

"But they will make me leave," Sally said anxiously.

"Don't be silly, Sally, I won't make you leave. You're staying here with us and we will get this sorted out."

"She needs to rest," said the doctor sternly.

Chapter Twelve

The Last Christmas of the War

The weather was bad and getting worse the sheep were in the top paddock and were suffering in the snow like all of us. We had to take hay up to them to keep them going while the snow was on the ground.

"Will you girls take the horse and the cart and fill it with hay and take it up to the sheep before dinner?"

"We will, George."

"I'll hitch her to the cart. You get the forks. Is that alright, Jenny?"

"Yes that's fine."

We made our way to the top of the field and started to fork out the hay.

"It's freezing up here I'll be glad when this is done. At least it's warm when we milk the cows."

"Steady, girl, steady, this track is freezing, we better take it slow."

"We've put Tess in the stable and the cart in the barn. The track from the top field is freezing."

"Better check the water main to make Sure it isn't frozen, Dolly."

"Yes, George, I will do."

We bedded up all the animals then checked all the water troughs then went into Gaynor for dinner.

"I'm ready for this today, Gaynor."

"Me, too."

We sat at the table and had a lovely bowl of cowl with cheese and bread. It's a Welsh dish that Gaynor makes when it's cold, it's filling and warm and very tasty.

"More, Dolly?"

"Yes please."

Dolly does have a good appetite and never seems to put weight on.

We all rallied round Sally and helped get things together. She booked in with the midwife and Pat began to do some knitting.

"Jenny I've found some of the girl's baby clothes and washed them. Do you think Sally will want them?" Gaynor said.

"That's very kind of you Gaynor she would appreciate it."

"How is she now?"

"Well I think she feels better now we all know, and that Tony is standing by her. Not that Pat would have given him any choice."

"She's due in two weeks. Pat has done the attic out, then the boys can go up there. It's a little low but they will love it, Sally will have the boys' old room, Pat has put the cot in already at the bottom of the bed."

"Do you think they will marry?" Gaynor said.

"Oh yes, they have been writing all the time but Sally just hadn't told him she was pregnant."

Sally was getting very tired and took to her bed and after a few days on the 17th September Rose Patricia was born. Pat was over the moon that it was a little girl. She was very proud of Sally who was very tired and had been told to spend ten days in bed. Mainly as she had done too much early on. Tony came home on leave and was smitten with Rose. Tony and Sally got engaged to Pat's relief and arrangements were made for them to get married. A Christmas wedding giving Sally time to recover after the birth. Sally was just glad she was marrying her Tony, it might not have started out the right way but they were a lovely little family. Tony had finished his allotted missions and had moved on to training the new crews. Pat and Sally were pleased about that.

"When does Tony start his leave Sally?" I asked

"The Thursday before the wedding then we have the Friday to sort out the last minute things."

"When's your family getting here?" Pat asked.

"Well only Mam and Dad can come and they arrive at the pub Friday," Sally said.

"It will be the first time they will see Rose and meet Tony. I'm so nervous."

"They can't help but like Tony; and Rose would melt anybody heart," I said.

"Yes she is a darling isn't she?"

"Let's hope this war will be over soon and she can grow up with her Mum and Dad with no memory of the war."

"I agree, Jenny, I hope this is the last Christmas of the war."

Tony arrived and the house was buzzing. All the Bell family were so pleased to be together. Mark and Philip enjoyed having their big brother around. It was good to see them together. Tony was so gentle with Rose and you could clearly see what his feelings for Sally were. The change in him since we first came was immense. Mark and Philip were seventeen and fifteen now and becoming really nice young men. Pat was longing for the war to be over before the boys were of age when they would have to be called up. Anyway back to the wedding weekend.

"Mark, answer that door will you?"

"Yes, Mam."

Sally's Mum and Dad had arrived at the pub and had made their way to Pat's.

"Hello, can I help?" said Mark.

"I hope so, lad, we're Sally's parents."

"Mark, who is it now?" Pat asked.

"It's Sally's Mum and Dad."

"Oh my god, boy, let them in."

"Alright."

"I'm sorry about that. I'm Pat, Tony's Mum, come by the fire you must be freezing. Mark, tell Sally her parents are here. She's just feeding Rose. How was the journey?"

"Cold," Sally's Mum said.

Pat could feel a bit of tension from Sally's Mum, but her Dad seemed nice.

"Mum, Dad."

Sally ran to her Dad who threw his arms around her. Her Mum was much more stand-offish to her.

"Well he's marrying you at least then is he?"

"Mum, don't start, please don't spoil it."

Tony came from the parlour with Rose in his arms and stood forward by Sally's side.

"Hello, I'm Tony and this is Rose your granddaughter. I know what has happened isn't what you wanted for Sally."

"We didn't say that, lad."

"I know we have done things the wrong way round but I love Sally and Sally loves me and we both don't regret Rose in any way."

"No, lad, we're sorry if it came across that way. It's just Sally's Mum always had a white wedding in mind for her and then grandchildren."

"Mum, Dad I love Tony very much and he and Rose have made me very happy."

"Well that's all that counts then, darling, come here."

Sally went to her Dad and they embraced. Sally looked at her Mum.

"Mum please."

Her Mum walked over to Sally and her Dad then put her arms around them both. They all had a little cry.

"Cup of tea anyone?" Pat asked.

"Oh yes please, Mrs Bell," Sally's Dad replied.

"Call me Pat, please."

Tony stepped forwards with Rose.

"Here you go, this is your granddaughter."

Sally's Mum took hold of Rose and more tears ran down her face. She put her arm around Tony then welcomed him to their family. That was it, all bad feelings had gone. We all chattered till late then Sally, Rose and her parents went over to the pub. Sally was staying at the pub with them and going to church from there. The next day was frantic. We all had great fun and danced till late into the night. The next morning we were all feeling a little hung over to say the least but we went to work anyway.

"Jenny, don't let me drink again. When Pat said it was a punch she wasn't kidding."

"I know I thought it was a fruit punch. I don't really drink that much."

We made our way to the midden. Georg was there sitting on a stool by one of the cows.

"You two look rough. It was a good wedding then I presume."

"Well we did have a little too much of Pat's punch. It was well named," I said.

"You two finish off here. Give you chance to sober up a bit before breakfast."

"Breakfast don't," Dolly said.

We both got on with the job in hand. George was right we did feel much better before we went into breakfast.

"Here you go, get this lot into you. You will feel much better after you have eaten."

"Thanks, Gaynor, I think?"

The rest of the day we did our best with our jobs on the farm. We were both glad when it was time to go home to Pat's.

After Tony had gone back to his barracks Sally and Rose settled themselves coming back down to earth without him. Sally started to sort things out for Rose's first Christmas. Pat was very excited she got the tree and was making paper chains.

"It's going to be grand having a little one about at Christmas this year."

"She's not big enough to remember anything," Dolly said.

"No but we are," said Pat.

We were all hoping that when D-day happened in the summer that it would be over by Christmas but it wasn't and it did leave a sombre mood over a lot of people. There were hardly any presents out there in the shops but we made the best of things. Marge came round to see us all. She was due to have her first baby any day now. Her and Sally were talking babies in the kitchen, when Dolly and I came in from the farm.

"Hello, Marge, how are you?"

"Tired and a bit fed up now."

"I bet you are, you're even bigger than when I saw you last week."

"I know I can hardly get up out of the chair."

"Has Paul got Christmas off this year?" I asked

"Yes he's got a week's leave with the baby being due. Sorry that will mean Peter will be working."

"I know he said last night, but I'll be at the farm till lunchtime anyway."

"Well I better be off home before it gets too dark for me to see where I am. If I don't see you before Christmas have a good one."

It was strange four young girls came to Sutton-on-Derwent three are now married one is a mother and another is about to be. The one I thought would have had a fella is still single since we lost Roddy. I spent the last few days before Christmas trying to sort out few bits of presents for everyone.

"The presents aren't much this year but there's nothing out there."

"Don't worry we've all had the same problem, Jenny."

"Christmas Day at last," Jill said as she ran into kitchen where we were all eating breakfast.

"What are you so excited about, Jill? Have you been good enough this year for Father Christmas to come?"

"I have, Jenny; I have been helping Dad with all his jobs, and getting logs for Mum."

"Well done, Jill, I hope you get what you want," I said.

"Thank you, Jenny. Shall I do the chickens Mum?"

"Yes, darling, but take your sister with you."

"She hates doing them. Can't I go on my own, she's in the parlour with grandma."

"Alright but take a bucket with you for the eggs."

"I will, Mum."

"She is so helpful I wish Millie was more like her. She hates doing anything on the farm," said Gaynor.

"What did you manage to get them for Christmas?" I asked.

"There wasn't much as you know so we went practical. We got a pony for Jill from a friend of George's. We did have the 'nothing gets on this farm without earning it's keep' speech but I told him I could use it to go in to the village and take the girls to school in the little trap as petrol is so short now. Then I bought Millie a Singer sewing machine from a friend of Edith who has arthritis and can't use it any longer. Good presents for the girls but I found it hard for any others."

We finished our breakfasts and went out and bedded up and fed the stock. We set up for milking tonight for George and got wood in for Gaynor, then went back in to the kitchen.

"Jill, Millie, come on into the kitchen, please."

The girls came in with Edith from the parlour to the kitchen. Gaynor had wrapped the Singer with George's newspapers and handed it over to Millie on the table.

"What's this Mum? I thought we had had our presents."

"This is a special one."

"Oh, Mum, that's fantastic. I will be able to make a dress, blouse and…"

"Steady on we'll have to find you some material first and collect the coupons."

"It's perfect, Mum, Dad, I am so pleased with it."

Jill was sitting by the fire looking quite solemn. There wasn't anything else on the table or any other parcels in the kitchen.

"Well, Jill, we will have to go outside for your present."

"Outside?"

"Yes."

Dolly had tacked up the pony to the cart and it was standing in the yard, Jill opened the door and squealed.

"Oh, a pony, a real live pony. Is she really mine?"

"Yes, Darling; she is yours, but Mum will use her to go to the village and take you to school, but you can ride her too. She has a saddle."

"Oh Mum, Dad she is really great can we go on her now?"

"Well we can take Dolly and Jenny home. I'll drive her but you can sit up front and watch what I do."

We had our drive home. It was lovely to see Jill and Millie's faces when they got their presents. You couldn't find two happier girls that Christmas Day.

"Merry Christmas, Pat, Sally."

"Hello, Jenny, Merry Christmas and to you, Dolly," Pat said.

"How's Rose, Sally?"

"She's good thanks and enjoying her first Christmas, Aren't you darling?"

"Well come on let's get sat at the table and have this Christmas dinner. Sorry it's not as good as other years, girls, but things are really getting short."

"I know, I do hope this is the last Christmas of the war."

"Well at least we are all safe at this moment in time. Let's make a toast to the end of the war."

We all repeated "to the end of the war". We tucked in to Pat's lovely meal. A knock came at the door.

"Well who on earth can that be on Christmas Day?" Dolly said.

I went to the door and Paul was stood there with his hand around Marge.

"Hello, you two, didn't expect to see you two today?"

"It's Marge. Her waters have gone. She's in labour."

"Come in, come in. Pat?"

Pat got up from the table and met us in the passage. She soon took in the scene and told Paul to take Marge upstairs to Pat's room.

"Why didn't you phone the midwife, Paul?" Pat asked?

"She's attending a difficult twin birth and doesn't know when she will be done. I told her where we would be, I didn't know where else to go, sorry, Pat."

"You did the right thing. Go in to the kitchen. Tell Philip to get you some food, and ask Mark to put some water on the range."

Dolly and I went upstairs with Pat to help make Marge as comfortable as we could.

"Right, Marge, you just relax now. How often are the pains?"

"Every five minutes and getting stronger since my waters broke."

"Good that's good. Won't be long now, Marge," Pat said.

Dolly went down to tell Paul. She asked him to go back home and fetch some of the baby's clothes.

"Don't be long."

"I won't," he ran out the back door.

Then at five thirty on Christmas Day Benjamin Philips was born. Marge was wonderful, a natural mother. Paul was speechless and couldn't stop thanking Marge for his son. Just after six pm the midwife arrived and checked Marge and Benjamin over. She couldn't believe how well Marge had done for a first time mother. We had some tea and sorted everything out from dinner that we had left. Paul slept on the sofa. We all went up to bed. This was definitely a Christmas we wouldn't forget in a long time.

Chapter Thirteen

The End is in Sight

The allied troops were pushing forward through France but tragically coming at a cost of many deaths and much destruction. The south of England had suffered attacks from Doodlebugs but we were to be grateful that we didn't have to continue with the blackouts. Churches were allowed to light up their stained glass windows. Such a simple thing you might think but it meant a lot to the people.

From October 1944 onwards there had been a significant return to the strategic bombing of Germany. The German fighter defences were short of fuel and had become generally ineffective despite the introduction of rocket-powered jet aircraft. The intensity of the strategic bombing effort was gratefully increased and many more sorties were flown but with a marked reduction in losses. We were beginning to hope the end was coming and that things would start to change. For the girls that had arrived in Elvinton in 1940 things had already changed so much.

"I can't believe we are milking one of the first calves we saw born, George. It's unbelievable," I said.

"I never thought we would be able to do this job when we first arrived that cold morning off the back of that lorry," Dolly said.

"I know, but we were so determined to show the locals that we could do it, we just did it."

"Well we couldn't have managed without you both this last few years. Trying everything I set you."

"Thanks, George, as we know the war will soon be over and we will have to leave you all and Pat."

"And each other," Dolly said.

Things at the base stated to change also, although Peter and Paul were still on radio operations for the French squadron. In March 1945 the Luftwaffe followed a returning bombing group straight back to their base. A Junkers ju88 was able to attack Elvington where the landing lights were switched on awaiting the French squadrons return. The aircraft came to grief in a low level attack some two kilometres from Elvington airfield. The plane crashed into a tree and then into a farm house. All four crew were killed and the two people that were on the farm.

"Hope Peter and Paul are alright. The airfield has been shut down all day I can't find anything out."

"Just keep calm. There's been no report of anyone being killed on the base," Pat said.

The farm where the Junkers had crashed was all cordoned off and there were four bodies covered beside the plane and another by the house near a tree. Two days later Peter and Paul both got leave. The base had been shot up a little by the Junker but nobody was injured. They had been cleaning up all the mess made and making the base operational again.

"Peter, I will be so glad when this is over. I thought you were safe on base."

"I'm safe don't worry. We will be together soon. We just have to be patient."

"What are we going to do after this war, and where are we going to live?"

"Well I don't want to go back to Blackburn. What about you?"

"Well Walton was quiet before the war. I don't think I'll fit in. I never did really."

"Well I know how you have really loved being on the farm with Gaynor and George. How would you feel about coming a farmer's wife?"

"What?"

"I've been talking to George and he knows of an old couple who want to retire and give it up. They only kept it going because of the war."

"How could we afford that, Peter, we have no money?"

"I have a trust fund, my Dad's sister never married and when she passed away she left her money for me and my brother. It was put in a trust fund as we were too young at the time."

"Why didn't you tell me when we got married?"

"I thought it would be a nice surprise for you after this damned war."

"Oh Peter, that would be wonderful. Have you been to see the farm yet?"

"No not yet, I was waiting till I told you. Then we could go together with George and Gaynor to help us give it the once over and to help us to come to a fair price with Mr Watt's."

"What about the things we don't know about?"

"George has already said he will help in any way."

We made arrangements to go to the farm when Peter got leave. We set off just after milking. There was a small but lovely farm house as you came into the farm yard. There were farm buildings on one side the barn and the byre on the other side, some pig sties and a small chicken hut. We walked over to the house, Mr Watt's came to the door to greet us.

"Hello, Ted, how are you?"

"Fine thanks, George; Gaynor, how's your mother?"

"Good thanks, she's got the girls."

"Well I better introduce you. This is Peter Shepard and his wife Jenny."

"Hello, nice to meet you both. Well I better show you round, I'll do the house first while we're clean."

We went in and were shown round the kitchen, parlour and then upstairs the three bedrooms. There was no bathroom of course and it wasn't large but large enough. It was well kept and very cosy.

"Peter I love it. It's so homely."

"I know we can be happy here."

"You two ready to go outside?"

"Yes we're ready."

We looked round the farm. The stock was going with the sale as Ted and Lil were retiring and moving in to a small cottage in the village. Ted would be giving us a hand at first when we took over.

"Well what do you think, is it right for you?" George asked.

"Yes it's just what we want, not too big and not too small, and with help from you and Ted I think we'll manage."

"Well we better go in and discus the price."

Everything was sorted out then we went back to George and Gaynor's, Peter and I said our goodbyes. I stayed at the farm to help George and Dolly do the afternoon milking.

"You look very pleased with yourself I suspect it went well."

"Yes it's wonderful I can't believe it, Dolly, our very own farm."

"You are so lucky, Jenny."

"Yes I know. I can't believe he kept it all from me, the trust and the farm but I'm so pleased he did."

We finished the milking and made our way home. I can't wait to tell Pat all about the farm and that I will be staying in Sutton-on-Derwent.

"Hello, Tony, didn't know you were getting leave."

"Well I didn't till the last minute. I think big things are happening, the final big push so we've got leave before it all starts."

"Bet you're pleased aren't you, Sally?"

"I wish he didn't have to go back though."

"Well I can see Rose is pleased to see Daddy," I said.

"Yes she is a real Daddy's girl. To say she hasn't got to see much of him she seems to know he's special to her."

Pat, Sally and Rose all enjoyed having Tony at home. We all prepared for more things to start to happen. In April it was looking much better for the Allied Forces. They were pushing forward. We were all getting really excited. You could feel that the end was in sight. The country was on edge and waiting for news overseas. The Soviet Army was unstoppable in its advance into Berlin, Hitler issued frantic orders to defend Berlin with armies that had already been wiped out or were making a hasty retreat to the west to the Americans. The end had come for Hitler, the Reich was a failure, and now there was nothing left for him to do but stay in Berlin and fight to the very end. On the night of April 27th a Soviet bombardment of the Chancellery Buildings where Hitler was, reached its peak with numerous direct hits. Of course we knew nothing of all this. We continued to work on the farm. Everyone was wondering what would happen next.

"I hope things are as near to the end as people seem to think," I said to Dolly as we milked the cows.

"What do you think you will do after the war, Dolly?"

"Well unlike you I didn't find my Mr Right or a lovely farm so I'll probably have to go back home."

"Have you thought about staying round here like Sally and I?"

"I would but, what would I do when the war is over? All the men will come home and want their jobs back."

"I know. It's going to be so strange seeing men about again not in uniform."

"Well I might at least get a man then."

"Ha, ha, ha!"

"Have you girls done? Breakfast is ready."

"Coming, Gaynor."

We went inside and sat at the table as it was a Saturday.

"Any more news on the wireless, George."

"Just waiting for a bulletin now. A special announcement is coming."

The announcement was made that Hitler had killed himself and his wife, Eva Broun, with more announcements to follow. It was great news to us all.

"Isn't it terrible we can all be so happy about someone killing themselves," said Edith.

"Well that's what war does and let's hope things come to an end soon."

We waited with baited breath for the war to end, and the end of six long hard years of suffering all over the world. The war ended on the seventh of May when Germany surrendered. On the eighth of May Britain's Prime Minister, Winston Churchill, made a broadcast announcing that the war in Europe was over. The news was fantastic; there was sadness but also relief. VE Day was finally here. We all celebrated. There were parties in the street and in the village hall. Bunting was all over the streets. Tables and chairs were placed in the streets everyone brought out any food they could. Children that had grown up knowing the war sat at the tables and celebrated.

"Dolly, are you ready. We're going."

"Yes coming, wait for me."

We were all going to the street party: All four of us girls that came here together. Peter and Paul were with us and Pat with Rose. We stayed out late that night.

"Oh Peter I can't believe it's finally over and we can have a normal life and a family of our own."

"I can't wait either, darling, just a few more weeks and they will begin demobbing people from the services."

"Yes and I hope we will soon hear from Tim. Then we can all be reunited."

The thought of seeing my brothers, Lilly and my Mum and Dad was a wonderful feeling; I couldn't wait till it happened.

Chapter Fourteen

Reunited at Last

The war was over, I couldn't believe it. There was still fighting going on in other parts of the world but no longer in Europe.

I was waiting for Peter to get his discharge papers that would say he had been demobbed. I would leave the farm at the end of the month. Mr and Mrs Watts had found a cottage in the village to rent and were sorting out the move. Ted was still working the farm till Peter and I were free to take over. It was so exciting the life we would be living. It would be hard though, knowing I would be leaving Gaynor, George and the farm.

"George that heifer's calving. I've put her in the barn. Shall I keep an eye on her?"

"Yes please, Jenny, but I want you there when she does. It's all good practice for you."

"Aright, George, I will."

"Dolly, Dolly where are you?" I shouted.

"In the pig pen."

"That heifer's calving and George wants me to keep an eye on her."

"Alright nearly done in here. Just need to put the swill in then I'm done."

We tidied up the yard and I kept an eye on the heifer. We collected the milk for Gaynor to make into butter then I went back in to check the heifer.

"George her bag's burst and there's two feet."

"Alright, coming."

We went in to the barn the heifer was struggling. George put her between the wall and a gate. He tied clean rope around the calves legs.

"Jenny, get hold of this one and I'll have the other, just put a little pressure on the rope and more when she strains."

"Alright, George."

"Steady, steady, girl, here it comes."

"Wow it's huge, George. No wonder she was struggling. That was a good trick with the two ropes, George."

"Dad taught me, it helps with just that bit of pressure. She doesn't get too tired with a lot of straining."

"Thanks George for letting me help. It's going to be hard when we go to the farm but what you have taught me over the last few years will be a big help."

"You'll be alright. We're only up the road, and Ted will be staying for a while."

People were coming home and families were being reunited those that could be. Tom and Lilly were both out of the RAF and were living with Mum and Dad, as there wasn't much room at the shop with John, Betty and their family. Peter had a date to be discharged. We were working up to the end of the month before moving into the farm, Ted and Lill were all ready to move out so I went up to give them a hand and to start to sort out the house by white-washing it all threw and sort out the furniture.

"Hello, Ted, you alright?"

"Yes thank you, Jenny, just putting the cows out, then we're ready."

"I'll go in and give Lill a hand."

"Alright."

"Hello, Lill, it's only me, Jenny."

"Hello, love, how are you?"

"Good can't wait to get in and start our marriage for real."

"I know you young ones have paid a big price for us to win this war."

"It will be good to have a normal life at last."

"I agree and for me and Ted to have a quieter retirement."

"What do you need me to do, Lill?"

"Well first I need to know how much furniture you have as we won't be able to take all ours with us as we will be downsizing somewhat and some will be too big to fit in the cottage."

"Well we have nothing really as we have never lived together."

"Well we'll leave everything we can't fit in. I know it is all dark wood and old but it will give you a bit of a start."

"Thanks Lill it will certainly help us."

We put the furniture they were taking on Ted's old cart and I had George's truck to help. We were finished by early afternoon and Ted stayed to milk at Elm Tree Farm. I took the truck back to George's and helped him finish off the milking.

It was my last day at the farm and it was very sad. I know I would only be next door but I would miss sitting round Gaynor's table and enjoying those lovely big breakfasts and lunches.

"Morning, Pat, you're up early."

"Well I thought I would get up with you, seeing as it is your last day at the farm. I know you will only be down the road but I have been used to having the house full of you girls."

"Well you will at least have Sally and Rose."

"Yes and Tony will be back next week."

"Oh that's wonderful you will have to come up to the farm were having a farm-warming to celebrate the start of our new life."

"That will be great all of us together."

"We're hoping to hear from Tim and when he will be back. I can't wait to see him. I won't believe he's alright till I see him."

"I can understand that. I won't believe Tony's here for good till he is actually here."

I had a cuppa with Pat and Dolly then I set off to the farm.

"It's going to be strange walking up here without you," Dolly said.

"Have you decided what you'll do? You'll be leaving soon."

"I know but I still don't know what to do when I leave."

It was a day much as any, but when it came to leaving Edith came out with the girls with presents, an embroidered tablecloth from Edith. It was beautiful. The girls had two little chicks to go in my little chicken hut and start my own brood.

"Thanks Edith, when did you do all this? It's beautiful."

"I've been doing it since you and Peter got married."

I hugged Edith and the girls and told them they must visit when they liked. Then Gaynor came out with tears in her eyes.

"Oh, Gaynor, don't start you'll set me off."

Gaynor gave me six napkins to match Edith's table cloth. She had handmade them. She also gave me provisions to take to the farm.

"Oh thank you, Gaynor, for everything. You need to come round to give me cooking lessons or Peter might starve."

"Ha, ha, ha."

George brought the truck round to help me with my belongings and my clothes from Pat's. We had much the same scene at Pat's, tears and presents. Mark and Philip made me a clothes basket out of reeds like they had made their Mum a couple of Christmases ago.

"Boy's I can't thank you enough. It has been like having my brothers with me the last few years and the presents will all come in handy." Then Pat came out with a box in her hands.

"What on earth?"

"It's not brand new, I got it from that bring and buy at the village hall."

I opened the box and underneath the tissue paper there was the most beautiful china tea service.

"Oh, Pat, that's wonderful and so pretty!"

"You're welcome and don't be a stranger."

"I won't."

I climbed back in to the truck with tears rolling down my face as we drove down the road to Elm Tree Farm.

"Well here we are girl. Your new life starts here."

George helped me in with all my belongings then we said our goodbyes.

"Don't forget, any worries give us a shout."

"Thanks, George, for everything."

"Get away with you; you're the one that should be being thanked and Dolly for all your help."

"You and Gaynor have helped to change our lives and for that I will always be grateful."

"When's Peter back?"

"The weekend I hope and don't forget the farm-warming."

"I won't."

George went. I just looked around my kitchen, and I couldn't believe it – my own kitchen. I put all the things away and lit the fire put on the kettle and had a sandwich. I went upstairs and made up the bed, and then I put on my boots and went to check the stock. Ted would be back up tomorrow to help me milk and show me the routine. Gaynor was coming late morning to show me how to make the butter and my first cooking lesson. I could cook the basics, but bread, jam and preserves I knew nothing of. I closed down the fire and went upstairs to bed. It was strange being on my own after being with Pat and the girls but Peter would be here the day after tomorrow and our life together would truly begin.

"Morning, Ted, want a cup before we start?"

"I never say no to a cuppa, girl."

We did the milking and Ted showed me where to leave the milk churns. We fed the stock and cleared up the entire yard.

"I'll go in and start on breakfast, Ted."

"Alright, Lass."

As I got back to the house and the postwoman was at the door.

"Hello, Jenny, settled in have you?"

"Well sort off."

"A letter came from your Mum, I knew you had left Pat's so I brought it up."

"Thank you, do you want a cuppa?"

"No thanks, not today but I will take a rain check."

"Alright."

The letter from Mum was just what I was waiting for.

Dear Jenny

Good news, Tim is in England. He's in a convalescence home, as he is very weak but alright. He will be there about a month then we will all come over to you for the farm-warming

you keep talking about. Hope you get this as I didn't know
whether to send it to Pat's or the farm. I will write with news
as soon as I have some. I'm going down with Tom and Lilly to
see him.

Love Mum

Well I couldn't believe it, Tim was back in England. All I needed was my Peter. It seemed to take ages waiting for the weekend to come but at last it was here. I was up early and milked with Ted and then after breakfast I did a big clean up and baked some bread. Gaynor had showed me how to do it, it wasn't as good as hers but I expected practice would make perfect. I watched the lane from the kitchen window willing Peter to come. I heard a truck and thought it must be George. No, it was Peter he was in a truck. I ran out onto the lane and Peter stopped the truck.

"Peter, darling, where did you get this from?"

"Dad has been saving it. He's been doing it up for us as a house warming present and we will need one."

"Oh, Peter, we are so lucky, I can't believe it."

We soon fell into the workings of the farm and with Ted's help it was getting easier. We arranged the big reunion and farm-warming. It was the day before and Pat and Gaynor were helping with food and putting up family we couldn't fit in. They were all coming from both sides of the family, eager to see the farm.

"Mum, Dad you found it alright?"

"Yes, darling, it's beautiful."

"Robert, old chap you look well how are you?"

"Good, brother, good, I'm taking over the garage and expanding it with Dad."

"Great, Dad needs the help. Well I better introduce you to my wife, and gosh that still sounds strange."

"I know – my baby brother all married and owning his own farm."

"Jenny, Jenny darling, this is Robert my big brother."

"Hello Jenny, we meet at last, I'm sorry I missed the wedding."

"Don't worry at least you are here now and safe."

We all chipped in and everything was ready for the party.

"I wish Mum and Dad would get here. I can't wait to see Tim."

"They won't be long. You know what the trains are like."

"Dolly you're here you look good."

"You look stressed."

"No, just anxious us about seeing Tim."

Friends and neighbours began to arrive. We introduced everyone.

"Hello Dolly I've heard a lot about you from Jenny in her letters."

"All good I hope," Dolly said.

"Ha, ha-ha."

I was talking to George and there was another knock on the door.

"I'll get it," Peter said.

I could hear laughing and back slapping going on from the kitchen then Peter shouted me through.

"Jenny, Jenny, there's someone here to see you."

I ran into the hall and Tim was standing by Peter. He looked very thin and older.

"Tim! Oh, Tim, is it really you?"

"Well I hope so, sis. Come here."

I ran to him and we embraced. I didn't want to let him go. Tom was there and Lilly, too.

"You all look fantastic. Mum, Dad it's so good to have you all here at the farm."

How all our lives have changed since 1939? Love, loss and being apart, we all ate the food that we had made. It was wonderful to catch up and all be reunited at last.

THE END